5 Ingredients

Diabetic Cookbook

1600 Days Affordable & Healthy Recipes with Balanced Diabetic Diet for Newly Diagnosed to Eat on A Healthy Diet

Cerys Johnson

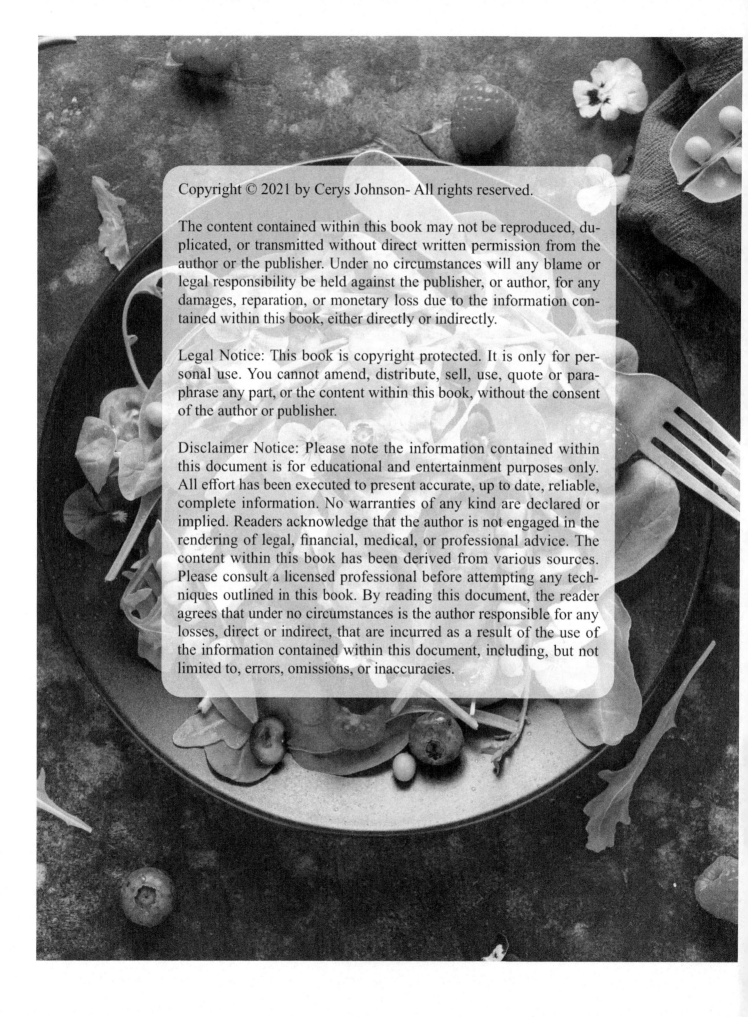

CONTENTS

Poultry Recipes 29

Meat Recipes 38

INTRODUCTION

I have married with my husband for twelve years. When I found out the news that he had diabetes, I was in disbelief and had no any idea what to do in this case totally. For all these years, my life is so peaceful and steady that I didn't think anything will change.

Unfortunately, after the long search, we found out that his diabetes is incurable. I started thinking how to take care of him. Diabetes has been a difficult disease to live with for my husband, and I've been there through all the highs and lows. There have been countless sleepless nights where I've had to wake up to check his blood sugar, social outings we couldn't go on because he was too tired or high on glucose, and medical bills that we couldn't afford...

One day I talked with the doctor, who told me the disease was not fatal, but what should we do to get better. The doctor told me that we should take care of our diet and exercise as well as following his instructions so as to avoid any complication. He said that if my husband gets treatment in time, he will have a normal life for many years. Hearing this, I felt relieved and grabbed the opportunity to make an effort for his recovery.

The silver lining has been our bond - we've grown closer than ever before and truly learned about what it means to be in such a tough situation together. He's learned how to fight back by managing his diabetes in different ways, while I helped with everything else. We tried different ways to manage it and to fight it.

Over time, we learned to live with diabetes. My husband is living like a healthy and normal person.

Diet and exercise is important, like our doctor said. I am the one in charge of his diet, so I decide to write a cookbook about our diabetes diet to help and give hopes to other diabetes diagnosed.

Diabetes Basics

Diabetes is a chronic or long-lasting disease that affects how your body turns food into energy. It is a disease that occurs when your blood glucose, or blood sugar, is too high. Blood sugar comes from the food you eat, which is also your main source of energy. Insulin, a hormone made by the pancreas, helps glucose from food get into your cells to be used for energy. Sometimes your body doesn't make enough insulin or can't use it as well as it should. Blood sugar will stays in your bloodstream.

Over time, having too much glucose in your blood can cause health problems, such as:

* heart disease

* stroke

* kidney disease

* eye problems

* dental disease

* nerve damage

* foot problems

There are three main and common types of diabetes: type 1, type 2, and gestational diabetes (diabetes while pregnant).

Although there is currently no treatment for diabetes, decreasing weight, eating well, and exercising can all be very beneficial. You can manage your diabetes and live a long, healthy life by taking good care of yourself everyday.

Nearly every aspect of your body can be impacted by diabetes. Therefore, you need to manage your blood glucose levels, also called blood sugar. Managing or controlling your blood glucose, as well as your blood pressure and cholesterol, can help prevent the health problems that can occur when you have diabetes.

So how to manage diabetes?

Your self-care plan may include the following suggestion but not limited:

Stop smoking

If you're a smoker, both smoking and diabetes narrow blood vessels, which increases burden on the heart and your heart will work harder. Even E-cigarettes aren't a safe option either.

Make exercise a regular part of your day

Set a goal to be more physically active. Try to work up to 30 minutes or more of exercise everyday or most days of the week.

Manag your stress well

When you live with diabetes, feeling stressed, sad, or angry is common. Stress will make your blood glucose levels go up, but you can learn methods to lower your stress. Try deep breathing, taking a walk, doing yoga, meditating, or listening to your favorite music.

Try to get enough sleep

Sleep apnea is common if you live with diabetes. If you often feel sleepy during the day, you may have obstructive sleep apnea, a condition in which your breathing briefly stops many times during the night. Talk with your doctor if you think you have a sleep problem. Getting enough sleep can help improve your mood and energy level.

Follow your diabetes meal plan

Make a diabetes meal plan is the most important step. Following a healthy meal plan and being active can help you keep your blood glucose level, also called blood sugar, in your target range. You may worry that you are unable to enjoy your favorite foods. The good thing is that you can still enjoy your favorite foods, but you will need to have them less often or in smaller amounts.

Keep in mind that managing diabetes is not easy, but it is worthwhile to live your healthiest life with diabetes.

Measurement Conversions

BASIC KITCHEN CONVERSIONS & EQUIVALENTS

DRY MEASUREMENTS CONVERSION CHART

3 TEASPOONS = 1 TABLESPOON = 1/16 CUP

6 TEASPOONS = 2 TABLESPOONS = 1/8 CUP

12 TEASPOONS = 4 TABLESPOONS = 1/4 CUP

24 TEASPOONS = 8 TABLESPOONS = 1/2 CUP

36 TEASPOONS = 12 TABLESPOONS = 3/4 CUP

48 TEASPOONS = 16 TABLESPOONS = 1 CUP

METRIC TO US COOKING CONVERSIONS

OVEN TEMPERATURES

120 °C = 250 °F

160 °C = 320 °F

180° C = 350 °F

205 °C = 400 °F

220 °C = 425 °F

LIQUID MEASUREMENTS CONVERSION CHART

8 FLUID OUNCES = 1 CUP = 1/2 PINT = 1/4 QUART

16 FLUID OUNCES = 2 CUPS = 1 PINT = 1/2 QUART

32 FLUID OUNCES = 4 CUPS = 2 PINTS = 1 QUART

 = 1/4 GALLON

128 FLUID OUNCES = 16 CUPS = 8 PINTS = 4 QUARTS = 1 GALLON

BAKING IN GRAMS

1 CUP FLOUR = 140 GRAMS

1 CUP SUGAR = 150 GRAMS

1 CUP POWDERED SUGAR = 160 GRAMS

1 CUP HEAVY CREAM = 235 GRAMS

VOLUME

1 MILLILITER = 1/5 TEASPOON

5 ML = 1 TEASPOON

15 ML = 1 TABLESPOON

240 ML = 1 CUP OR 8 FLUID OUNCES

1 LITER = 34 FL. OUNCES

WEIGHT

1 GRAM = .035 OUNCES

100 GRAMS = 3.5 OUNCES

500 GRAMS = 1.1 POUNDS

1 KILOGRAM = 35 OUNCES

US TO METRIC COOKING CONVERSIONS

1/5 TSP = 1 ML

1 TSP = 5 ML

1 TBSP = 15 ML

1 FL OUNCE = 30 ML

1 CUP = 237 ML

1 PINT (2 CUPS) = 473 ML

1 QUART (4 CUPS) = .95 LITER

1 GALLON (16 CUPS) = 3.8 LITERS

1 OZ = 28 GRAMS

1 POUND = 454 GRAMS

BUTTER

1 CUP BUTTER = 2 STICKS = 8 OUNCES = 230 GRAMS = 8 TABLESPOONS

WHAT DOES 1 CUP EQUAL

1 CUP = 8 FLUID OUNCES

1 CUP = 16 TABLESPOONS

1 CUP = 48 TEASPOONS

1 CUP = 1/2 PINT

1 CUP = 1/4 QUART

1 CUP = 1/16 GALLON

1 CUP = 240 ML

BAKING PAN CONVERSIONS

1 CUP ALL-PURPOSE FLOUR = 4.5 OZ

1 CUP ROLLED OATS = 3 OZ 1 LARGE EGG = 1.7 OZ

1 CUP BUTTER = 8 OZ 1 CUP MILK = 8 OZ

1 CUP HEAVY CREAM = 8.4 OZ

1 CUP GRANULATED SUGAR = 7.1 OZ

1 CUP PACKED BROWN SUGAR = 7.75 OZ

1 CUP VEGETABLE OIL = 7.7 OZ

1 CUP UNSIFTED POWDERED SUGAR = 4.4 OZ

BAKING PAN CONVERSIONS

9-INCH ROUND CAKE PAN = 12 CUPS

10-INCH TUBE PAN = 16 CUPS

11-INCH BUNDT PAN = 12 CUPS

9-INCH SPRINGFORM PAN = 10 CUPS

9 X 5 INCH LOAF PAN = 8 CUPS

9-INCH SQUARE PAN = 8 CUPS

Breakfast Recipes

Whole Wheat Buttermilk Rolls

Servings: 6 | Cooking Time: 45 Minutes

Ingredients:
- 1 1/2 cups self-rising flour
- 1 1/2 cups whole wheat flour
- 1/3 cup sugar
- 1 package (1/4 ounce) quick-rise yeast
- 1 cup buttermilk
- 1/4 cup canola oil

Directions:

1. In a large bowl, combine the self-rising flour, 3/4 cup whole wheat flour, sugar and yeast. In a small saucepan, heat buttermilk and oil to 120°-130° (mixture will appear curdled). Add to dry ingredients; beat just until smooth. Stir in remaining whole wheat flour.
2. Turn onto a lightly floured surface; knead until smooth and elastic, about 6-8 minutes. Cover and let dough rest for 10 minutes.
3. Roll dough to 1/2-in. thickness; cut with a floured 2 1/2-in. biscuit cutter. Place 2 in. apart on baking sheets coated with cooking spray. Cover and let rise in a warm place until doubled, about 35-40 minutes.
4. Bake at 375° for 8-12 minutes or until golden brown. Serve warm.

Nutrition Info:
- 116 cal., 3 g fat (trace sat. fat), 1 mg chol., 135 mg sodium, 19 g carb., 1 g fiber, 3 g pro.

English Muffin Melts

Servings: 8 | Cooking Time:3 Minutes

Ingredients:
- 4 whole-wheat English muffins, cut in half
- 2 tablespoons reduced-fat mayonnaise
- 3 ounces sliced reduced-fat Swiss cheese, torn in small pieces
- 4 ounces oven-roasted deli turkey, finely chopped

Directions:

1. Preheat the broiler.
2. Arrange the muffin halves on a baking sheet and place under the broiler for 1–2 minutes or until lightly toasted. Remove from broiler and spread 3/4 teaspoon mayonnaise over each muffin half.
3. Arrange the cheese pieces evenly on each muffin half and top with the turkey.
4. Return to the broiler and cook 3 minutes, or until the turkey is just beginning to turn golden and the cheese has melted.

Nutrition Info:
- 120 cal., 3g fat (1g sag. fat), 15mg chol, 290mg sod., 15g carb (3g sugars, 2g fiber), 9g pro.

Blackberry Smoothies

Servings:4 | Cooking Time: 10 Minutes

Ingredients:

- 1 cup orange juice
- 1 cup (8 ounces) plain yogurt
- 2 to 3 tablespoons honey
- 1 1/2 cups fresh or frozen blackberries
- 1/2 cup frozen unsweetened mixed berries
- Additional blackberries and yogurt, optional

Directions:

1. In a blender, combine the first five ingredients; cover and process for about 15 seconds or until smooth. Pour into chilled glasses; serve immediately. If desired top with additional blackberries and yogurt.

Nutrition Info:

- 130 cal., 2g fat (1g sat. fat), 8mg chol., 29mg sod., 26g carb. (21g sugars, 3g fiber), 3g pro.

Double-duty Banana Pancakes

Servings: 8 | Cooking Time:6 Minutes

Ingredients:

- 2 ripe medium bananas, thinly sliced
- 1 cup buckwheat pancake mix
- 3/4 cup plus 2 tablespoons fat-free milk
- 4 tablespoons light pancake syrup

Directions:

1. Mash one half of the banana slices and place in a medium bowl with the pancake mix and the milk. Stir until just blended.
2. Place a large nonstick skillet over medium heat until hot. (To test, sprinkle with a few drops of water. If the water drops "dance" or jump in the pan, it's hot enough.) Coat the skillet with nonstick cooking spray, add two scant 1/4 cup measures of batter, and cook the pancakes until puffed and dry around the edges, about 1 minute.
3. Flip the pancakes and cook until golden on the bottom. Place on a plate and cover to keep warm.
4. Recoat the skillet with nonstick cooking spray, add three scant 1/4 cup measures of batter, and cook as directed. Repeat with the remaining batter.
5. Place 2 pancakes on each of 4 dinner plates, top with equal amounts of banana slices, and drizzle evenly with the syrup. If you like, place the dinner plates in a warm oven and add the pancakes as they are cooked.

Nutrition Info:

- 100 cal., 0g fat (0g sag. fat), 0mg chol, 140mg sod., 23g carb (9g sugars, 2g fiber), 3g pro.

Orange-honey Yogurt

Servings:1 | Cooking Time:7 Minutes

Ingredients:

- 1 cup 2 percent Greek yogurt
- 2 tablespoons honey
- ¼ teaspoon grated orange zest plus 2 tablespoons juice

Directions:

1. Whisk ingredients together in bowl. (Yogurt can be refrigerated for up to 3 days.) Serve.

Nutrition Info:

- 15 cal., 0g fat (0g sag. fat), 0mg chol., 0mg sod., 2g carb (2g sugars, 0g fiber), 1g pro.

Scrambled Eggs With Herbs

Servings:2 | Cooking Time:x

Ingredients:

- 4 large eggs
- 2 teaspoons 1 percent low-fat milk
- Pinch salt
- Pinch pepper
- 1 teaspoon extra-virgin oil
- 2 tablespoons minced fresh chives, basil, and tarragon

Directions:

1. Beat eggs, milk, salt, and pepper with fork in bowl until eggs are thoroughly combined and color is pure yellow; do not overbeat.
2. Heat oil in 10-inch nonstick skillet over medium-high heat until shimmering, swirling to coat pan. Add egg mixture and, using rubber spatula, constantly and firmly scrape along bottom and sides of skillet until eggs begin to clump and spatula just leaves trail on bottom of pan, 45 to 75 seconds. Reduce heat to low and gently but constantly fold eggs until clumped and just slightly wet, 30 to 60 seconds. Quickly fold in herbs, then immediately transfer eggs to individual warmed plates. Serve immediately.

Nutrition Info:

- 170 cal., 12g fat (3g sag. fat), 370mg chol, 220mg sod., 1g carb (1g sugars, 0g fiber), 13g pro.

Popcorn With Olive Oil

Servings:14 | Cooking Time:10 Minutes

Ingredients:

- 1 tablespoon water
- ½ cup popcorn kernels
- 2 tablespoons extra-virgin olive oil
- ½ teaspoon salt
- ½ teaspoon pepper

Directions:

1. Heat Dutch oven over medium-high heat for 2 minutes. Add water and popcorn, cover, and cook, shaking frequently, until first few kernels begin to pop. Continue to cook, shaking vigorously, until popping slows to about 2 seconds between pops. Transfer popcorn to large serving bowl and toss with oil, salt, and pepper. Serve.

Nutrition Info:

- 90 cal., 4g fat (0g sag. fat), 0mg chol, 170mg sod., 10g carb (0g sugars, 2g fiber), 1g pro.

Good Morning Power Parfait

Servings: 4 | Cooking Time: 5 Minutes

Ingredients:

- 1 ripe medium banana
- 2 cups fat-free, artificially sweetened, vanilla-flavored yogurt (divided use)
- 1 teaspoon ground cinnamon
- 1 cup whole strawberries, sliced
- 1/2 cup grape-nut-style cereal, preferably with raisins and almonds

Directions:

1. Add the banana, 1 cup yogurt, and 1 teaspoon cinnamon, if desired, to a blender and blend until smooth. Pour into 4 wine or parfait glasses.
2. Top each parfait with 1/4 cup sliced strawberries, 1/4 cup yogurt, and 2 tablespoons cereal.

Nutrition Info:

- 140 cal., 0g fat (0g sag. fat), 0mg chol, 125mg sod., 32g carb (14g sugars, 3g fiber), 5g pro.

Spinach And Feta Omelets

Servings:2 | Cooking Time:10 Minutes

Ingredients:

- 4 large eggs
- 1 tablespoon canola oil
- 1 shallot, minced
- 4 ounces (4 cups) baby spinach
- 1 ounce feta cheese, crumbled (¼ cup)

Directions:

1. Beat 2 eggs with fork in bowl until eggs are thoroughly combined and color is pure yellow; do not overbeat. Repeat with remaining 2 eggs in second bowl.
2. Heat 1 teaspoon oil in 10-inch nonstick skillet over medium heat until shimmering. Add shallot and cook until softened, about 2 minutes. Stir in spinach and cook until wilted, about 1 minute. Using tongs, squeeze out any excess moisture from spinach mixture, then transfer to bowl and cover to keep warm. Wipe skillet clean with paper towels and let cool slightly.
3. Heat 1 teaspoon oil in now-empty skillet over medium heat until shimmering. Add 1 bowl of eggs and cook until edges begin to set, 2 to 3 seconds. Using rubber spatula, stir eggs in circular motion until slightly thickened, about 10 seconds. Use spatula to pull cooked edges of eggs in toward center, then tilt skillet to 1 side so that uncooked eggs run to edge of skillet. Repeat until omelet is just set but still moist on surface, 20 to 25 seconds. Sprinkle 2 tablespoons feta and half of spinach mixture across center of omelet.
4. Off heat, use spatula to fold lower third (portion nearest you) of omelet over filling; press gently with spatula to secure seam, maintaining fold. Run spatula between outer edge of omelet and skillet to loosen. Pull skillet sharply toward you few times to slide unfolded edge of omelet up far side of skillet. Jerk skillet again so that unfolded edge folds over itself, or use spatula to fold edge over. Invert omelet onto plate. Tidy edges with spatula and serve immediately.
5. Wipe skillet clean with paper towels and repeat with remaining 1 teaspoon oil, remaining eggs, remaining 2 tablespoons feta, and remaining filling.

Nutrition Info:

- 270 cal., 20g fat (6g sag. fat), 385mg chol, 320mg sod., 6g carb (2g sugars, 2g fiber), 16g pro.

Breakfast Grilled Swiss Cheese And Rye

Servings: 2 | Cooking Time:7 Minutes

Ingredients:

- 2 slices rye bread
- 4 teaspoons reduced-fat margarine (35% vegetable oil)
- 2 large eggs
- 1 1/2 ounces sliced, reduced-fat Swiss cheese, torn in small pieces

Directions:

1. Spread one side of each bread slice with 1 teaspoon margarine and set aside.
2. Place a medium skillet over medium heat until hot. Coat with nonstick cooking spray and add the egg substitute. Cook 1 minute without stirring. Using a rubber spatula, lift up the edges to allow the uncooked portion to run under. Cook 1–2 minutes longer or until eggs are almost set and beginning to puff up slightly. Flip and cook 30 seconds.
3. Remove the skillet from the heat and spoon half of the eggs on the unbuttered sides of two of the bread slices. Arrange equal amounts of the cheese evenly over each piece.
4. Return the skillet to medium heat until hot. Coat the skillet with nonstick cooking spray. Add the two sandwiches and cook 3 minutes. If the cheese doesn't melt when frying the sandwich bottom, put it under the broiler until brown. Using a serrated knife, cut each sandwich in half.

Nutrition Info:

- 250 cal., 13g fat (4g sag. fat), 200mg chol, 360mg sod., 17g carb (2g sugars, 2g fiber), 16g pro.

Morning Cinnamon Rolls

Servings: 8 | Cooking Time: 25 Minutes

Ingredients:

- 1 tube (8 ounces) refrigerated reduced-fat crescent rolls
- 1/2 teaspoon ground cinnamon
- Sugar substitute equivalent to 1/2 cup sugar, divided
- 1/4 cup confectioners' sugar
- 1 tablespoon fat-free milk

Directions:

1. Unroll crescent dough into a rectangle; seal seams and perforations. Combine the cinnamon and half of the sugar substitute; sprinkle over dough. Roll up jelly-roll style, starting with a long side; seal edge. Cut into eight slices.
2. Place rolls cut side down in a 9-in. round baking pan coated with cooking spray. Bake at 375° for 12-15 minutes or until golden brown.
3. In a small bowl, combine the confectioners' sugar, milk and remaining sugar substitute; drizzle over warm rolls.
4. TO FREEZE Cool unfrosted rolls and wrap in foil. Freeze for up to 3 months.
5. TO USE FROZEN ROLLS Thaw at room temperature; warm if desired. Follow directions for icing.

Nutrition Info:

- 123 cal., 5 g fat (1 g sat. fat), trace chol., 234 mg sodium, 18 g carb., trace fiber, 2 g pro.

Sweet Onion Frittata With Ham

Servings: 4 | Cooking Time:8 Minutes

Ingredients:

- 4 ounces extra-lean, low-sodium ham slices, chopped
- 1 cup thinly sliced Vidalia onion
- 1 1/2 cups egg substitute
- 1/3 cup shredded, reduced-fat, sharp cheddar cheese

Directions:

1. Place a medium nonstick skillet over medium-high heat until hot. Coat the skillet with nonstick cooking spray, add ham, and cook until beginning to lightly brown, about 2–3 minutes, stirring frequently. Remove from skillet and set aside on separate plate.
2. Reduce the heat to medium, coat the skillet with nonstick cooking spray, add onions, and cook 4 minutes or until beginning to turn golden, stirring frequently.
3. Reduce the heat to medium low, add ham to the onions, and cook 1 minute (this allows the flavors to blend and the skillet to cool slightly before the eggs are added). Pour egg substitute evenly over all, cover, and cook 8 minutes or until puffy and set.
4. Remove the skillet from the heat, sprinkle cheese evenly over all, cover, and let stand 3 minutes to melt the cheese and develop flavors.

Nutrition Info:

- 110 cal., 2g fat (1g sag. fat), 20mg chol, 460mg sod., 6g carb (4g sugars, 0g fiber), 17g pro.

Honey Wheat Breadsticks

Servings: 16 | Cooking Time: 40 Minutes

Ingredients:

- 1 1/3 cups water (70° to 80°)
- 3 tablespoons honey
- 2 tablespoons canola oil
- 1 1/2 teaspoons salt
- 2 cups bread flour
- 2 cups whole wheat flour
- 3 teaspoons active dry yeast

Directions:

1. In bread machine pan, place all ingredients in order suggested by manufacturer. Select dough setting (check dough after 5 minutes of mixing; add 1 to 2 tablespoons of water or flour if needed.
2. When cycle is completed, turn dough onto a lightly floured surface. Divide into 16 portions; shape each into a ball. Roll each into an 8-in. rope. Place 2 in. apart on greased baking sheets.
3. Cover and let rise in a warm place until doubled, about 30 minutes. Bake at 375° for 10-12 minutes or until golden brown. Remove to wire racks.

Nutrition Info:

- 131 cal., 2 g fat (trace sat. fat), 0 chol., 222 mg sodium, 25 g carb., 2 g fiber, 4 g pro.

Peach Cranberry Quick Bread

Servings: 14 | Cooking Time:45 Minutes

Ingredients:

- 1 (15.6-ounce) box cranberry quick bread and muffin mix
- 1 cup water
- 1/2 cup egg substitute or 4 large egg whites
- 2 tablespoons canola oil
- 2 cups chopped frozen and thawed unsweetened peaches

Directions:

1. Preheat the oven to 375°F.
2. Coat a nonstick 9 × 5-inch loaf pan with nonstick cooking spray.
3. Beat the bread mix, water, egg substitute, and oil in a medium bowl for 50 strokes or until well blended. Stir in the peaches and spoon into the loaf pan. Bake 45 minutes or until a wooden toothpick comes out clean.
4. Place the loaf pan on a wire rack for 20 minutes before removing the bread from the pan. Cool completely for peak flavor and texture.

Nutrition Info:

- 150 cal., 3g fat (0g sag. fat), 0mg chol, 150mg sod., 29g carb (15g sugars, 1g fiber), 3g pro.

Cheesy Mushroom Omelet

Servings: 2 | Cooking Time:6 Minutes

Ingredients:

- 6 ounces sliced mushrooms
- 1/8 teaspoon black pepper
- 1/3 cup finely chopped green onion (green and white parts)
- 1 cup egg substitute
- 2 tablespoons crumbled bleu cheese (about 1/4 cup) or 1/4 cup shredded, reduced-fat, sharp cheddar cheese

Directions:

1. Place a small skillet over medium-high heat until hot. Coat with nonstick cooking spray and add mushrooms and pepper. Coat the mushrooms with nonstick cooking spray and cook 4 minutes or until soft, stirring frequently.
2. Add the onions and cook 1 minute longer. Set the pan aside.
3. Place another small skillet over medium heat until hot. Coat with nonstick cooking spray and add the egg substitute. Cook 1 minute without stirring. Using a rubber spatula, lift up the edges to allow the uncooked portion to run under. Cook 1–2 minutes longer or until eggs are almost set and beginning to puff up slightly.
4. Spoon the mushroom mixture on one half of the omelet, sprinkle the cheese evenly over the mushrooms, and gently fold over. Cut in half to serve.

Nutrition Info:

- 110 cal., 2g fat (1g sag. fat), 5mg chol, 340mg sod., 6g carb (3g sugars, 1g fiber), 16g pro.

Yogurt Parfaits

Servings:4 | Cooking Time:8 Minutes

Ingredients:

- 1 cup whole almonds, toasted and chopped
- ½ cup raw sunflower seeds, toasted
- 3 cups low-fat plain yogurt
- 20 ounces (4 cups) blackberries, blueberries, raspberries, and/or sliced strawberries

Directions:

1. Combine almonds and sunflower seeds in bowl. Using four 16-ounce glasses, spoon ¼ cup yogurt into each glass, then top with ⅓ cup berries, followed by 2 tablespoons nut mixture. Repeat layering process 2 more times with remaining yogurt, berries, and nut mixture. Serve.

Nutrition Info:

- 480 cal., 29g fat (4g sag. fat), 10mg chol, 130mg sod., 39g carb (24g sugars, 11g fiber), 22g pro.

Quick Veggie Frittata

Servings: 4 | Cooking Time: 20 Minutes

Ingredients:

- 4 whole eggs
- 6 egg whites
- ¾ teaspoon Italian seasoning
- ¼ teaspoon salt
- Dash pepper
- 2 teaspoons canola or olive oil
- 2 cups frozen Italian-blend vegetables, thawed (from 1-lb bag)
- 2 tablespoons shredded Parmesan cheese

Directions:

1. In medium bowl, beat whole eggs, egg whites, Italian seasoning, salt and pepper until well mixed.
2. In 10-inch skillet, heat oil over medium heat. Pour egg mixture into skillet; top with vegetables. Reduce heat to medium-low. Cook 3 to 4 minutes, lifting eggs with spatula to allow uncooked portion to flow to bottom.
3. Cover; cook 7 to 8 minutes longer or until eggs are almost set but top is slightly moist. Top with cheese. Cover; cook 1 to 2 minutes or until cheese is melted.

Nutrition Info:

- 150 cal., 9g fat (2.5g sat. fat), 215 chol., 360mg sod., 4g carb. (2g sugars, 1g fiber), 14g pro.

Sausage Potato Skillet Casserole

Servings: 4 | Cooking Time:17 Minutes

Ingredients:

- 5 ounces reduced-fat, smoked turkey sausage, kielbasa style
- 2 cups chopped onion
- 4 cups frozen hash brown potatoes with peppers and onions
- 1/3 cup shredded, reduced-fat, sharp cheddar cheese

Directions:

1. Cut the sausage in fourths lengthwise. Cut each piece of sausage in 1/4-inch pieces.
2. Place a large nonstick skillet over medium-high heat until hot. Coat the skillet with nonstick cooking spray, add sausage, and cook 3 minutes or until the sausage begins to brown, stirring frequently. Set the sausage aside on a separate plate.
3. Recoat the skillet with nonstick cooking spray, add the onions, and cook 5 minutes or until the onions begin to brown, stirring frequently.
4. Reduce the heat to medium, add the frozen potatoes and sausage, and cook 9 minutes or until the potatoes are lightly browned, stirring occasionally.
5. Remove the skillet from the heat, top with cheese, cover, and let stand 5 minutes to melt the cheese and develop flavors.

Nutrition Info:

- 190 cal., 5g fat (2g sag. fat), 25mg chol, 450mg sod., 26g carb (5g sugars, 4g fiber), 9g pro.

Appetizers And Snacks Recipes

Zippy Tortilla Chips

Servings: 2 | Cooking Time: 20 Minutes

Ingredients:
- 1/2 teaspoon brown sugar
- 1/4 teaspoon garlic powder
- 1/4 teaspoon onion powder
- 1/4 teaspoon ground cumin
- 1/4 teaspoon paprika
- 1/8 teaspoon cayenne pepper
- 4 corn tortillas (6 inches)
- Cooking spray

Directions:

1. In a small bowl, combine the first six ingredients. Stack the tortillas; cut into six wedges. Arrange in a single layer on a baking sheet coated with cooking spray.
2. Spritz the wedges with cooking spray; sprinkle with seasoning mixture. Bake at 375° for 9-10 minutes or until lightly browned. Cool for 5 minutes.

Nutrition Info:
- 138 cal., 3 g fat (trace sat. fat), 0 chol., 85 mg sodium, 26 g carb., 3 g fiber, 3 g pro.

Dilled Chex Toss

Servings: 18 | Cooking Time:30 Minutes

Ingredients:
- 6 cups multi-grain or Wheat Chex cereal
- 4-ounce packet ranch salad dressing mix
- 1 tablespoon dried dill
- 2 tablespoons extra virgin olive oil

Directions:
1. Preheat the oven to 175°F.
2. Place the cereal, dressing mix, and dill in a large zippered plastic bag. Seal and shake gently to blend well.
3. Place the mixture on a large rimmed baking sheet or jelly roll pan, drizzle the oil evenly over all, and stir thoroughly to blend. Spread out in a single layer and bake 30 minutes or until browned lightly, stirring once.

Nutrition Info:
- 50 cal., 1g fat (0g sag. fat), 0mg chol, 200mg sod., 8g carb (1g sugars, 1g fiber), 1g pro.

Creamy Peaches

Servings: 4 | Cooking Time: 10 Minutes

Ingredients:

- 1 can (15 ounces) sliced peaches in extra-light syrup, drained
- 1 1/2 cups (12 ounces) fat-free cottage cheese
- 4 ounces fat-free cream cheese, cubed
- Sugar substitute equivalent to 1 tablespoon sugar

Directions:

1. Thinly slice four peach slices; set aside for garnish. Place remaining peaches in a food processor; add the cottage cheese. Cover and process until blended. Add cream cheese and sugar substitute; cover and process until blended.
2. Spoon into four serving dishes. Top with reserved peaches. Refrigerate until serving.

Nutrition Info:

- 127 cal., trace fat (trace sat. fat), 6 mg chol., 443 mg sodium, 15 g carb., 1 g fiber, 15 g pro.

Sausage & Salsa Breakfast Burritos

Servings: 6 | Cooking Time: 20 Minutes

Ingredients:

- 5 breakfast turkey sausage links
- 2 cartons (8 ounces each) egg substitute
- 1/2 cup salsa
- 1/4 teaspoon pepper
- 6 whole wheat tortilla (8 inches), warmed
- 1/2 cup shredded reduced-fat cheddar cheese

Directions:

1. Cook sausage links according to package directions. Meanwhile, in a large bowl, whisk the egg substitute, salsa and pepper. Pour into a large nonstick skillet coated with cooking spray. Cook and stir over medium heat until eggs are nearly set. Chop the sausage links. Add to egg mixture; cook and stir until completely set.
2. Spoon 1/3 cup egg mixture off center on each tortilla and sprinkle with 4 teaspoons cheese. Fold sides and ends over filling and roll up.

Nutrition Info:

- 265 cal., 10 g fat (3 g sat. fat), 25 mg chol., 602 mg sodium, 25 g carb., 2 g fiber, 18 g pro.

Basil Spread And Water Crackers

Servings: 4 | Cooking Time: 5 Minutes

Ingredients:

- 2 ounces reduced-fat garlic and herb cream cheese
- 1/2 cup finely chopped fresh basil
- 12 fat-free water crackers

Directions:

1. Stir the cream cheese and basil together in a small bowl until well blended.
2. Place 1 teaspoon spread on each cracker.

Nutrition Info:

- 70 cal., 2g fat (1g sag. fat), 0mg chol, 200mg sod., 9g carb (1g sugars, 0g fiber), 3g pro.

Peppered Pork Pitas

Servings: 4 | Cooking Time: 20 Minutes

Ingredients:

- 1 pound boneless pork loin chops, cut into thin strips
- 1 tablespoon olive oil
- 2 teaspoons coarsely ground pepper
- 2 garlic cloves, minced
- 1 jar (12 ounces) roasted sweet red peppers, drained and julienned
- 4 whole pita breads, warmed

Directions:

1. In a small bowl, combine the pork, oil, pepper and garlic; toss to coat. In a large skillet, saute pork mixture until no longer pink. Add red peppers; heat through. Serve with pita breads.

Nutrition Info:

- 380 cal., 11 g fat (3 g sat. fat), 55 mg chol., 665 mg sodium, 37 g carb., 2 g fiber, 27 g pro.

Tuna Salad Stuffed Eggs

Servings: 4 | Cooking Time:10 Minutes

Ingredients:

- 4 large eggs
- 1 (2.6-ounce) packet tuna (or 5-ounce can of tuna packed in water, rinsed and well drained)
- 2 tablespoons reduced-fat mayonnaise
- 1 1/2–2 tablespoons sweet pickle relish

Directions:

1. Place eggs in a medium saucepan and cover with cold water. Bring to a boil over high heat, then reduce the heat and simmer 10 minutes.
2. Meanwhile, stir the tuna, mayonnaise, and relish together in a small bowl.
3. When the eggs are cooked, remove them from the water and let stand one minute before peeling under cold running water. Cut eggs in half, lengthwise, and discard 4 egg yolk halves and place the other 2 egg yolk halves in the tuna mixture and stir with a rubber spatula until well blended. Spoon equal amounts of the tuna mixture in each of the egg halves.
4. Serve immediately, or cover with plastic wrap and refrigerate up to 24 hours.

Nutrition Info:

- 90 cal., 4g fat (1g sag. fat), 105mg chol, 240mg sod., 3g carb (2g sugars, 0g fiber), 9g pro.

Lime'd Blueberries

Servings: 6 | Cooking Time: 5 Minutes

Ingredients:

- 2 cups frozen unsweetened blueberries, partially thawed
- 1/4 cup frozen grape juice concentrate
- 1 1/2 tablespoons lime juice

Directions:

1. Place all ingredients in a medium bowl and toss gently.
2. Serve immediately for peak flavor and texture.

Nutrition Info:

- 50 cal., 0g fat (0g sag. fat), 0mg chol, 5mg sod., 13g carb (11g sugars, 1g fiber), 0g pro.

Minutesi Feta Pizzas

Servings:4 | Cooking Time: 20 Minutes

Ingredients:

- 2 whole wheat English muffins, split and toasted
- 2 tablespoons reduced-fat cream cheese
- 4 teaspoons prepared pesto
- 1/2 cup thinly sliced red onion
- 1/4 cup crumbled feta cheese

Directions:

1. Preheat oven to 425°. Place muffins on a baking sheet.
2. Mix cream cheese and pesto; spread over muffins. Top with onion and feta cheese. Bake until lightly browned, 6-8 minutes.

Nutrition Info:

- 136 cal., 6g fat (3g sat. fat), 11mg chol., 294mg sod., 16g carb. (4g sugars, 3g fiber), 6g pro.

Mocha Pumpkin Seeds

Servings:3 | Cooking Time: 25 Minutes

Ingredients:

- 6 tablespoons sugar
- 2 tablespoons baking cocoa
- 1 tablespoon instant coffee granules
- 1 large egg white
- 2 cups salted shelled pumpkin seeds (pepitas)

Directions:

1. Preheat oven to 325°. Place sugar, cocoa and coffee granules in a small food processor; cover and pulse until finely ground.
2. In a bowl, whisk egg white until frothy. Stir in pumpkin seeds. Sprinkle with sugar mixture; toss to coat evenly. Spread in a single layer in a parchment paper-lined 15x10x1-in. baking pan.
3. Bake 20-25 minutes or until dry and no longer sticky, stirring seeds every 10 minutes. Cool completely in pan. Store in an airtight container.

Nutrition Info:

- 142 cal., 10g fat (2g sat. fat), 0 chol., 55mg sod., 10g carb. (7g sugars, 1g fiber), 6g pro.

Sparkling Party Punch

Servings: 5 | Cooking Time: 17 Minutes

Ingredients:

- 1 can (46 ounces) unsweetened pineapple juice, chilled
- 3 cups apricot nectar or juice, chilled
- 1 liter diet lemon-lime soda, chilled
- Pineapple sherbet, optional

Directions:

1. In a punch bowl, combine the pineapple juice, apricot nectar and soda. Top with scoops of sherbet if desired. Serve immediately.

Nutrition Info:

- 66 cal., trace fat (trace sat. fat), 0 chol., 9 mg sodium, 16 g carb., trace fiber, trace pro.

Asparagus Ham Roll-ups

Servings: 16 | Cooking Time: 25 Minutes

Ingredients:

- 16 fresh asparagus spears, trimmed
- 1 medium sweet red pepper, cut into 16 strips
- 8 ounces Havarti cheese, cut into 16 strips
- 8 thin slices deli ham or prosciutto, cut in half lengthwise
- 16 whole chives

Directions:

1. In a large skillet, bring 1 in. of water to a boil. Add asparagus; cover and cook for 3 minutes. Drain and immediately place asparagus in ice water. Drain and pat dry.
2. Place an asparagus spear, red pepper strip and cheese strip on each piece of ham. Roll up tightly; tie with a chive. Refrigerate until serving.

Nutrition Info:

- 69 cal., 5 g fat (3 g sat. fat), 18 mg chol., 180 mg sodium, 2 g carb., trace fiber, 6 g pro.

Cucumber Punch

Servings: 25 | Cooking Time: 15 Minutes

Ingredients:

- 2 medium cucumbers
- 3 cups water
- 1 can (12 ounces) frozen lemonade concentrate, thawed
- 2 liters diet ginger ale, chilled
- 4 1/2 cups diet grapefruit or citrus soda, chilled

Directions:

1. With a zester or fork, score cucumbers lengthwise; cut widthwise into thin slices. In a large pitcher, combine water and lemonade concentrate; add cucumbers. Cover and refrigerate overnight.
2. Just before serving, transfer cucumber mixture to a punch bowl; stir in ginger ale and grapefruit soda.

Nutrition Info:

- 29 cal., trace fat (trace sat. fat), 0 chol., 15 mg sodium, 7 g carb., trace fiber, trace pro.

Tropical Treats

Servings: 4 | Cooking Time: 5 Minutes

Ingredients:
- 2 cups (16 ounces) reduced-fat plain yogurt
- 1 can (8 ounces) unsweetened crushed pineapple, drained
- 2 teaspoons sugar
- 1/4 teaspoon coconut extract
- 1/4 teaspoon grated lime peel

Directions:

1. In a small bowl, combine all ingredients. Chill until serving.

Nutrition Info:
- 121 cal., 2 g fat (1 g sat. fat), 7 mg chol., 86 mg sodium, 20 g carb., trace fiber, 7 g pro.

Bleu Cheese'd Pears

Servings: 4 | Cooking Time: 5 Minutes

Ingredients:
- 2 ounces fat-free cream cheese
- 3 1/2 tablespoons crumbled bleu cheese
- 2 medium firm pears, halved, cored, and sliced into 20 slices

Directions:

1. In a small bowl, microwave the cheeses on HIGH for 10 seconds to soften. Use a rubber spatula to blend well.
2. Top each pear slice with 3/4 teaspoon cheese.
3. To prevent the pear slices from discoloring, toss them with a tablespoon of orange, pineapple, or lemon juice. Shake off the excess liquid before topping them with cheese.

Nutrition Info:
- 90 cal., 2g fat (1g sag. fat), 10mg chol, 190mg sod., 14g carb (9g sugars, 3g fiber), 4g pro.

Turkey Reubens

Servings: 4 | Cooking Time: 25 Minutes

Ingredients:
- 8 slices rye bread
- 1/2 pound thinly sliced deli turkey
- 1/2 cup sauerkraut, rinsed and well drained
- 4 slices reduced-fat Swiss cheese
- 1/4 cup fat-free Thousand Island salad dressing

Directions:

1. On four slices of bread, layer the turkey, sauerkraut, cheese and salad dressing. Top with remaining bread. Spritz both sides of sandwiches with butter-flavored cooking spray.
2. In a large nonstick skillet over medium heat, toast sandwiches on both sides until cheese is melted.

Nutrition Info:
- 310 cal., 8 g fat (3 g sat. fat), 35 mg chol., 1,398 mg sodium, 39 g carb., 5 g fiber, 22 g pro.

Tortellini Appetizers

Servings: 6 | Cooking Time: 25 Minutes

Ingredients:

- 18 refrigerated cheese tortellini
- 1/4 cup fat-free Italian salad dressing
- 6 thin slices (4 ounces) reduced-fat provolone cheese
- 6 thin slices (2 ounces) Genoa salami
- 18 large pimiento-stuffed olives

Directions:

1. Cook tortellini according to package directions; drain and rinse in cold water. In a resealable plastic bag, combine tortellini and salad dressing. Seal bag and refrigerate for 4 hours.
2. Place a slice of cheese on each slice of salami; roll up tightly. Cut into thirds. Drain tortellini and discard dressing. For each appetizer, thread a tortellini, salami roll-up and olive on a toothpick.

Nutrition Info:

- 92 cal., 6 g fat (3 g sat. fat), 16 mg chol., 453 mg sodium, 5 g carb., trace fiber, 7 g pro.

Crostini With Kalamata Tomato

Servings: 4 | Cooking Time:10 Minutes

Ingredients:

- 4 ounces multigrain baguette bread, cut in 12 slices (about 1/4 inch thick)
- 1 small tomato, finely chopped
- 9 small kalamata olives, pitted and finely chopped
- 2 tablespoons chopped fresh basil

Directions:

1. Preheat the oven to 350°F.
2. Arrange the bread slices on a baking sheet and bake 10 minutes or until just golden on the edges. Remove from the heat and cool completely.
3. Meanwhile, stir the remaining ingredients together in a small bowl. Spread 1 tablespoon of the mixture on each bread slice.

Nutrition Info:

- 90 cal., 2g fat (0g sag. fat), 0mg chol, 220mg sod., 16g carb (2g sugars, 1g fiber), 3g pro.

Goat Cheese Crostini

Servings: 16 | Cooking Time: 10 Minutes

Ingredients:

- 1 cup crumbled goat cheese
- 1 teaspoon minced fresh rosemary
- 1 French bread baguette (10 1/2 ounces), cut into 1/2-inch slices and toasted
- 3 tablespoons honey
- 1/4 cup slivered almonds, toasted

Directions:

1. In a small bowl, combine cheese and rosemary; spoon over toast slices. Drizzle with honey; sprinkle with almonds.
2. BACON-ALMOND CROSTINI Combine 2 cups shredded Monterey Jack cheese, 2/3 cup mayonnaise, 1/2 cup toasted sliced almonds, 6 slices crumbled cooked bacon, 1 chopped green onion and a dash of salt. Spread over toast. Bake for 5-7 minutes or until cheese is melted. Sprinkle with additional almonds if desired.

Nutrition Info:

- 76 cal., 4 g fat (2 g sat. fat), 6 mg chol., 92 mg sodium, 9 g carb., 1 g fiber, 3 g pro.

Fruit Smoothies

Servings: 4 | Cooking Time: 10 Minutes

Ingredients:

- 2 cups 2% milk
- 1 cup frozen unsweetened sliced peaches
- 1 cup frozen unsweetened strawberries
- 1/4 cup orange juice
- 2 tablespoons honey

Directions:

1. In a blender, combine all ingredients. Cover and process until smooth. Pour into chilled glasses; serve immediately.

Nutrition Info:

- 128 cal., 2 g fat (1 g sat. fat), 9 mg chol., 62 mg sodium, 23 g carb., 1 g fiber, 5 g pro.

Bird's Nest Breakfast Cups

Servings: 6 | Cooking Time: 30 Minutes

Ingredients:
- 12 turkey bacon strips
- 1 1/2 cups egg substitute
- 6 tablespoons shredded reduced-fat Mexican cheese blend
- 1 tablespoon minced fresh parsley

Directions:

1. In a large skillet, cook bacon over medium heat for 2 minutes on each side or until partially set but not crisp. Coat six muffin cups with cooking spray; wrap two bacon strips around the inside of each cup. Fill each with 1/4 cup egg substitute; top with cheese.
2. Bake at 350° for 18-20 minutes or until set. Cool for 5 minutes before removing from pan. Sprinkle with the parsley.

Nutrition Info:
- 120 cal., 7 g fat (2 g sat. fat), 30 mg chol., 515 mg sodium, 2 g carb., trace fiber, 12 g pro.

Pineapple Iced Tea

Servings: 5 | Cooking Time: 10 Minutes

Ingredients:
- 4 cups water
- 7 individual tea bags
- 1 cup unsweetened pineapple juice
- 1/3 cup lemon juice
- 2 tablespoons sugar

Directions:

1. In a large saucepan, bring water to a boil. Remove from the heat.
2. Add tea bags; cover and steep for 3-5 minutes. Discard tea bags. Stir in the pineapple juice, lemon juice and sugar until sugar is dissolved. Refrigerate overnight for the flavors to blend. Serve over ice.

Nutrition Info:
- 51 cal., 0 fat (0 sat. fat), 0 chol., 1 mg sodium, 13 g carb., 0 fiber, 0 pro.

Poultry Recipes

Lemon Chicken With Olives

Servings: 4 | Cooking Time: 20 Minutes

Ingredients:

- 4 boneless skinless chicken breast halves (about 1¼ lb)
- 2 teaspoons olive or canola oil
- 1 tablespoon lemon juice
- 1 teaspoon salt-free lemon-pepper seasoning
- ¼ cup sliced ripe olives
- 4 thin slices lemon

Directions:

1. Set oven control to broil. Spray broiler pan rack with cooking spray. Starting at thickest edge of each chicken breast, cut horizontally almost to opposite side. Open cut chicken breast so it is an even thickness.
2. In small bowl, mix oil and lemon juice. Drizzle over both sides of chicken breasts. Sprinkle both sides with lemon-pepper seasoning. Place on rack in broiler pan.
3. Broil with tops 4 inches from heat about 10 minutes, turning once, until chicken is no longer pink in center. During last 2 minutes of broiling, top with olives and lemon slices.

Nutrition Info:

- 200 cal., 8g fat (1.5g sat. fat), 85 chol., 150mg sod., 1g carb. (0g sugars, 0g fiber), 31g pro.

Turkey & Apricot Wraps

Servings:4 | Cooking Time: 15 Minutes

Ingredients:

- 1/2 cup reduced-fat cream cheese
- 3 tablespoons apricot preserves
- 4 whole wheat tortillas (8 inches), room temperature
- 1/2 pound sliced reduced-sodium deli turkey
- 2 cups fresh baby spinach or arugula

Directions:

1. In a small bowl, mix cream cheese and preserves. Spread about 2 tablespoons over each tortilla to within 1/2 in. of edges. Layer with turkey and spinach. Roll up tightly. Serve immediately or wrap in plastic wrap and refrigerate until serving.

Nutrition Info:

- 312 cal., 10g fat (4g sat. fat), 41mg chol., 655mg sod., 33g carb. (8g sugars, 2g fiber), 20g pro.

Peach Barbecued Chicken

Servings: 4 | Cooking Time:18 Minutes

Ingredients:

- 8 chicken drumsticks, skin removed, rinsed and patted dry (about 2 pounds total)
- 2 tablespoons peach all-fruit spread
- 1/4 cup barbeque sauce, preferably hickory- or mesquite-flavored
- 2 teaspoons grated gingerroot

Directions:

1. Preheat the broiler.
2. Coat a broiler rack and pan with nonstick cooking spray. Arrange the drumsticks on the rack and broil about 4 inches away from heat source for 8 minutes. Turn and broil 6 minutes or until the juices run clear.
3. Meanwhile, place the fruit spread in a small glass bowl and microwave on HIGH 20 seconds or until the fruit spread has melted slightly. Add the barbeque sauce and ginger and stir to blend. Place 1 tablespoon of the mixture in a separate small bowl and set aside.
4. When the chicken is cooked, brush with half of the sauce and broil 2 minutes. Turn the drumsticks, brush with the remaining half of the sauce, and broil 2 more minutes.
5. Remove the drumsticks from the broiler, turn them over, and brush with the reserved 1 tablespoon sauce to serve.

Nutrition Info:

- 230 cal., 6g fat (1g sag. fat), 95mg chol, 220mg sod., 13g carb (10g sugars, 0g fiber), 29g pro.

Cranberry-glazed Turkey Breast

Servings: 12 | Cooking Time: 110 Minutes

Ingredients:

- 1 1/4 cups jellied cranberry sauce
- 2/3 cup thawed unsweetened apple juice concentrate
- 2 tablespoons butter
- 1 bone-in turkey breast (5 to 6 pounds)

Directions:

1. In a small saucepan, bring the cranberry sauce, apple juice concentrate and butter to a boil. Remove from the heat; cool.
2. Carefully loosen skin of turkey breast. Set aside 1/2 cup sauce for basting and 3/4 cup for serving. Spoon remaining sauce onto the turkey, rubbing mixture under and over skin.
3. Place turkey on a rack in a shallow roasting pan. Bake, uncovered, at 325° for 1 1/2 to 2 hours or until a thermometer reads 170°, basting occasionally with reserved sauce. Cover and let stand for 10 minutes before carving. Warm reserved 3/4 cup of sauce; serve with turkey.

Nutrition Info:

- 244 cal., 3 g fat (1 g sat. fat), 103 mg chol., 91 mg sodium, 17 g carb., trace fiber, 36 g pro.

Avocado And Green Chili Chicken

Servings: 4 | Cooking Time:22 Minutes

Ingredients:

- 4 (4 ounces each) boneless, skinless chicken breast, flattened to 1/2-inch thickness
- 1 (4-ounce) can chopped mild green chilies
- 1 ripe medium avocado, chopped
- 1 lime, halved

Directions:

1. Preheat oven to 400°F.
2. Place chicken in an 11 × 7-inch baking pan, squeeze half of the lime over all. Spoon green chilies on top of each breast and spread over all. Bake, uncovered, 22–25 minutes or until chicken is no longer pink in center.
3. Top with avocado, squeeze remaining lime half over all, and sprinkle evenly with 1/4 teaspoon salt and 1/4 teaspoon pepper.

Nutrition Info:

- 200 cal., 8g fat (1g sag. fat), 85mg chol, 310mg sod., 6g carb (1g sugars, 3g fiber), 27g pro.

Chicken Apple Sausage And Onion Smothered Grits

Servings: 4 | Cooking Time:10 Minutes

Ingredients:

- 2/3 cup dry quick cooking grits
- 8 ounces sliced fresh mushrooms
- 3 (4 ounces each) links fully cooked chicken apple sausage, thinly sliced, such as Al Fresco
- 1 1/2 cups chopped onion

Directions:

1. Bring 2 2/3 cups water to a boil in a medium saucepan. Slowly stir in the grits, reduce heat to medium-low, cover, and cook 5–7 minutes or until thickened.
2. Meanwhile, heat a large skillet coated with cooking spray over medium-high heat. Add the mushrooms and cook 4 minutes or until beginning to lightly brown. Set aside on separate plate.
3. Coat skillet with cooking spray and cook sausage 3 minutes or until browned on edges, stirring occasionally. Set aside with mushrooms. To pan residue, add onions, coat with cooking spray, and cook 4 minutes or until richly browned. Add the sausage and mushrooms back to the skillet with any accumulated juices and 1/4 cup water. Cook 1 minute to heat through.
4. Sprinkle with 1/8 teaspoon salt and 1/8 teaspoon pepper. Spoon equal amounts of the grits in each of 4 shallow soup bowls, top with the sausage mixture.

Nutrition Info:

- 270 cal., 7g fat (1g sag. fat), 60mg chol, 430mg sod., 31g carb (4g sugars, 3g fiber), 19g pro.

Turkey Patties With Dark Onion Gravy

Servings: 4 | Cooking Time:20 Minutes

Ingredients:

- 1 pound 93% lean ground turkey
- 1 tablespoon flour
- 1 1/3 cups chopped yellow onion
- 1 tablespoon sodium-free chicken bouillon granules

Directions:

1. Shape the turkey into 4 patties, about 1/2 inch thick; sprinkle with 1/8 teaspoon salt and 1/8 teaspoon pepper, if desired.
2. Heat a large skillet over medium-high heat. Add flour and cook 3 minutes or until beginning to lightly brown, stirring constantly. Set aside on separate plate.
3. Coat skillet with cooking spray, add onions, and cook 3 minutes or until beginning to brown on edges. Push to one side of the skillet, add the turkey patties, reduce to medium heat, and cook 6 minutes on each side or until no longer pink in center.
4. Remove the turkey patties from the onion mixture and set aside on serving platter. Add 1 cup water and bouillon granules to the onions, sprinkle with the flour and 1/8 teaspoon salt and 1/8 teaspoon pepper. Stir and cook until thickened, about 1 1/2 to 2 minutes. Spoon over patties.

Nutrition Info:

- 210 cal., 10g fat (2g sag. fat), 84mg chol, 230mg sod., 8g carb (2g sugars, 1g fiber), 22g pro.

Turkey With Cranberry Sauce

Servings: 15 | Cooking Time: 240 Minutes

Ingredients:

- 2 boneless skinless turkey breast halves (3 pounds each)
- 1 can (14 ounces) jellied cranberry sauce
- 1/2 cup plus 2 tablespoons water, divided
- 1 envelope onion soup mix
- 2 tablespoons cornstarch

Directions:

1. Place turkey breasts in a 5-qt. slow cooker. In a large bowl, combine the cranberry sauce, 1/2 cup water and soup mix. Pour over turkey. Cover and cook on low for 4-6 hours or meat is tender. Remove turkey and keep warm.
2. Transfer cooking juices to a large saucepan. Combine the cornstarch and remaining water until smooth. Bring cranberry mixture to a boil; gradually stir in cornstarch mixture until smooth. Cook and stir for 2 minutes or until thickened. Slice turkey; serve with cranberry sauce.

Nutrition Info:

- 248 cal., 1 g fat (trace sat. fat), 112 mg chol., 259 mg sodium, 12 g carb., trace fiber, 45 g pro.

Panko Ranch Chicken Strips With Dipping Sauce

Servings: 4 | Cooking Time: 12 Minutes

Ingredients:

- 8 chicken tenderloins, about 1 pound total
- 3/4 cup yogurt ranch dressing, divided use
- 3/4 cup panko breadcrumbs
- 3 tablespoons canola oil

Directions:

1. Place chicken in a medium bowl with 1/4 cup of the ranch dressing; toss until well coated. Place the breadcrumbs in a shallow pan, such as a pie pan. Coat chicken pieces, one at a time with the breadcrumbs and set aside.
2. Heat oil in a large skillet over medium-high heat. Add the chicken and immediately reduce to medium-low heat, cook 12 minutes or until golden and no longer pink in center, gently turning occasionally.
3. Remove from skillet, sprinkle with 1/8 teaspoon salt. Serve with remaining 1/2 cup ranch for dipping.

Nutrition Info:

- 340 cal., 16g fat (2g sag. fat), 85mg chol, 390mg sod., 17g carb (4g sugars, 1g fiber), 30g pro.

Easy Roast Turkey Breast

Servings: 12 | Cooking Time: 30 Minutes

Ingredients:

- 1 (5-pound) bone-in turkey breast
- ¼ cup salt
- 1 teaspoon pepper

Directions:

1. To remove backbone, use kitchen shears to cut through ribs following vertical line of fat where breast meets back, from tapered end of breast to wing joint. Using your hands, bend back away from breast to pop shoulder joint out of socket. With paring knife, cut through joint between bones to separate back from breast; discard backbone. Trim excess fat from breast. Dissolve salt in 4 quarts cold water in large container. Submerge turkey breast in brine, cover, and refrigerate for at least 3 hours or up to 6 hours.
2. Adjust oven rack to middle position and heat oven to 425 degrees. Set V-rack inside roasting pan and spray with vegetable oil spray. Remove turkey from brine, pat dry with paper towels, and sprinkle with pepper. Place turkey, skin side up, on prepared V-rack and add 1 cup water to pan. Roast turkey for 30 minutes.
3. Reduce oven temperature to 325 degrees and continue to roast until turkey registers 160 degrees, about 1 hour. Transfer turkey to carving board and let rest for 20 minutes. Carve turkey, discard skin, and serve.

Nutrition Info:

- 170 cal., 2g fat (0g sag. fat), 85mg chol, 310mg sod., 0g carb (0g sugars, 0g fiber), 35g pro.

Cheesy Chicken And Rice

Servings: 4 | Cooking Time:12 Minutes

Ingredients:

- 1 1/2 cups water
- 1 cup instant brown rice
- 12 ounces frozen broccoli and cauliflower florets
- 12 ounces boneless, skinless chicken breast, rinsed and patted dry, cut into bite-sized pieces
- 3 ounces reduced-fat processed cheese (such as Velveeta), cut in 1/2-inch cubes

Directions:

1. Bring the water to boil in a large saucepan, then add the rice and vegetables. Return to a boil, reduce the heat, cover tightly, and simmer 10 minutes or until the liquid is absorbed.
2. Meanwhile, place a large nonstick skillet over medium heat until hot. Coat the skillet with nonstick cooking spray and add the chicken. Cook 10 minutes or until the chicken is no longer pink in the center and is just beginning to lightly brown on the edges, stirring frequently.
3. Add the chicken, cheese, 1/8 teaspoon salt, if desired, and pepper to the rice mixture and stir until the cheese has melted. Add pepper to taste, if desired.

Nutrition Info:

- 340 cal., 6g fat (1g sag. fat), 55mg chol, 380mg sod., 43g carb (4g sugars, 4g fiber), 28g pro.

Chicken Sausages With Peppers

Servings: 4 | Cooking Time: 30 Minutes

Ingredients:

- 1 small onion, halved and sliced
- 1 small sweet orange pepper, julienned
- 1 small sweet red pepper, julienned
- 1 tablespoon olive oil
- 1 garlic clove, minced
- 1 package (12 ounces) fully cooked apple chicken sausage links or flavor of your choice, cut into 1-inch pieces

Directions:

1. In a large nonstick skillet, saute onion and peppers in oil until crisp-tender. Add garlic; cook 1 minute longer. Stir in sausages; heat through.

Nutrition Info:

- 208 cal., 11 g fat (2 g sat. fat), 60 mg chol., 483 mg sodium, 14 g carb., 1 g fiber, 15 g pro.

Smoked Turkey Breast

Servings:12 | Cooking Time:x

Ingredients:

- 1 (5-pound) bone-in turkey breast
- ¼ cup salt
- 1 teaspoon pepper
- 2 cups wood chips
- 1 (13 by 9-inch) disposable aluminum roasting pan (if using charcoal)

Directions:

1. To remove backbone, use kitchen shears to cut through ribs following vertical line of fat where breast meets back, from tapered end of breast to wing joint. Using your hands, bend back away from breast to pop shoulder joint out of socket. With paring knife, cut through joint between bones to separate back from breast; discard backbone. Trim excess fat from breast. Dissolve salt in 4 quarts cold water in large container. Submerge turkey breast in brine, cover, and refrigerate for at least 3 hours or up to 6 hours.

2. Just before grilling, soak wood chips in water for 15 minutes, then drain. Using large piece of heavy-duty aluminum foil, wrap soaked chips in foil packet and cut several vent holes in top. Remove turkey from brine, pat dry with paper towels, and sprinkle with pepper. Poke skin all over with skewer.

3. FOR A CHARCOAL GRILL Open bottom vent halfway and place disposable pan in center of grill. Light large chimney starter filled with charcoal briquettes (6 quarts). When top coals are partially covered with ash, pour into 2 even piles on either side of disposable pan. Place wood chip packet on coals. Set cooking grate in place, cover, and open lid vent halfway. Heat grill until hot and wood chips are smoking, about 5 minutes.

4. FOR A GAS GRILL Remove cooking grate and place wood chip packet directly on primary burner. Set cooking grate in place, turn all burners to high, cover, and heat grill until hot and wood chips are smoking, about 15 minutes. Turn all burners to medium-low. (Adjust burners as needed to maintain grill temperature around 350 degrees.)

5. Clean and oil cooking grate. Place turkey breast, skin side up, in center of grill (over disposable pan if using charcoal). Cover (position lid vent over turkey if using charcoal) and cook until skin is well browned and breast registers 160 degrees, about 1½ hours.

6. Transfer turkey to carving board and let rest for 20 minutes. Carve turkey, discard skin, and serve.

Nutrition Info:

- 170 cal., 2g fat (0g sag. fat), 85mg chol, 310mg sod., 0g carb (0g sugars, 0g fiber), 35g pro.

Honey-of-a-meal Chicken

Servings: 4 | Cooking Time: 30 Minutes

Ingredients:
- 4 bone-in chicken breast halves, skin removed (8 ounces each)
- 2 tablespoons olive oil
- 1 medium onion, finely chopped
- 1 cup chicken broth
- 2 tablespoons spicy brown mustard
- 1/2 teaspoon pepper
- 2 tablespoons honey

Directions:

1. In a pressure cooker, brown chicken breasts in oil in batches. Set chicken aside. Saute onion in the drippings until tender. Stir in the broth, mustard and pepper. Return chicken to the pan. Close cover securely according to manufacturer's directions.
2. Bring cooker to full pressure over high heat. Reduce heat to medium-high and cook for 8 minutes. (Pressure regulator should maintain a slow steady rocking motion or release of steam; adjust heat if needed.) Immediately cool according to manufacturer's directions until the pressure is completely reduced. Remove chicken and keep warm.
3. Stir honey into sauce. Bring to a boil. Reduce heat; simmer, uncovered, for 8-10 minutes or until thickened. Serve with the chicken.

Nutrition Info:
- 314 cal., 11 g fat (2 g sat. fat), 103 mg chol., 433 mg sodium, 13 g carb., 1 g fiber, 38 g pro.

Molasses Drumsticks With Soy Sauce

Servings: 4 | Cooking Time:25 Minutes

Ingredients:
- 2 1/2 tablespoons lite soy sauce
- 1 1/4 tablespoons lime juice
- 8 chicken drumsticks, skin removed, rinsed, and patted dry
- 2 tablespoons dark molasses

Directions:

1. Stir the soy sauce and lime juice together in a small bowl until well blended.
2. Place the drumsticks in a large zippered plastic bag. Add 2 tablespoons of the soy sauce mixture to the bag. Seal tightly and shake back and forth to coat chicken evenly. Refrigerate overnight or at least 2 hours, turning occasionally.
3. Add the molasses to the remaining soy sauce mixture, cover with plastic wrap, and refrigerate until needed.
4. Preheat the broiler. Lightly coat the broiler rack and pan with nonstick cooking spray, place the drumsticks on the rack, and discard any marinade in the bag. Broil 6 inches away from the heat source for 25 minutes, turning every 5 minutes or until the drumsticks are no longer pink in the center.
5. Place the drumsticks in a large bowl. Stir the reserved soy sauce mixture and pour it over the drumsticks. Toss the drumsticks gently to coat evenly and let them stand 3 minutes to develop flavors.

Nutrition Info:
- 210 cal., 6g fat (1g sag. fat), 95mg chol, 450mg sod., 6g carb (4g sugars, 0g fiber), 30g pro.

Meat Recipes

Berry Barbecued Pork Roast

Servings: 12 | Cooking Time: 75 Minutes

Ingredients:

- 1 boneless rolled pork loin roast (3 pounds)
- 1/4 teaspoon salt
- 1/4 teaspoon pepper
- 4 cups fresh or frozen cranberries
- 1 cup sugar
- 1/2 cup orange juice
- 1/2 cup barbecue sauce

Directions:

1. Sprinkle roast with salt and pepper. Place with fat side up on a rack in a shallow roasting pan. Bake, uncovered, at 350° for 45 minutes.
2. Meanwhile, in a saucepan, combine the cranberries, sugar, orange juice and barbecue sauce. Bring to a boil. Reduce heat to medium-low; cook and stir for 10-12 minutes or until cranberries pop and sauce is thickened.
3. Brush some of the sauce over roast. Bake 15-20 minutes longer or until a thermometer reads 145°, brushing often with sauce. Let meat stand for 10 minutes before slicing. Serve with remaining sauce.

Nutrition Info:

- 262 cal., 8 g fat (3 g sat. fat), 67 mg chol., 190 mg sodium, 23 g carb., 1 g fiber, 24 g pro.

Pan-seared Sirloin Steak

Servings:4 | Cooking Time:30 Seconds

Ingredients:

- 1 (1-pound) boneless beef top sirloin steak, 1 to 1½ inches thick, trimmed of all visible fat
- ¼ teaspoon salt
- ⅛ teaspoon pepper
- 2 teaspoons canola oil
- Lemon wedges

Directions:

1. Pat steak dry with paper towels and sprinkle with salt and pepper. Heat oil in 12-inch skillet over medium-high heat until just smoking. Brown steak well on first side, 3 to 5 minutes.
2. Flip steak and continue to cook until meat registers 120 to 125 degrees (for medium-rare), 5 to 10 minutes, reducing heat as needed to prevent scorching. Transfer steak to carving board, tent with aluminum foil, and let rest for 5 minutes. Slice steak thin and serve with lemon wedges.

Nutrition Info:

- 170 cal., 7g fat (2g sag. fat), 70mg chol, 210mg sod., 0g carb (0g sugars, 0g fiber), 25g pro.

Spicy Chili'd Sirloin Steak

Servings: 4 | Cooking Time: 11 Minutes

Ingredients:

- 1 pound boneless sirloin steak, trimmed of fat
- 2 tablespoons chili seasoning (available in packets)
- 1/8 teaspoon salt

Directions:

1. Coat both sides of the sirloin with the chili seasoning mix, pressing down so the spices adhere. Let stand 15 minutes, or overnight in the refrigerator for a spicier flavor (let steak stand at room temperature 15 minutes before cooking).
2. Place a large nonstick skillet over medium-high heat until hot. Coat the skillet with nonstick cooking spray, add the beef, and cook 5 minutes. Turn the steak, reduce the heat to medium, cover tightly, and cook 5 minutes. Do not overcook. Remove the skillet from the heat and let stand 2 minutes, covered.
3. Sprinkle the steak with salt and cut into 1/4-inch slices. Pour any accumulated juices over the steak slices.

Nutrition Info:

- 140 cal., 4g fat (1g sag. fat), 40mg chol, 250mg sod., 2g carb (0g sugars, 0g fiber), 23g pro.

Grilled Rosemary Lamb Chops

Servings: 2 | Cooking Time: 25 Minutes

Ingredients:

- 1 tablespoon country-style Dijon mustard
- 1 tablespoon chopped fresh rosemary
- 2 teaspoons honey
- 1 clove garlic, finely chopped
- ½ teaspoon salt
- ¼ teaspoon coarse ground black pepper
- 6 French-cut baby lamb chops (1 to 1¼ inches thick)

Directions:

1. Heat gas or charcoal grill. In small bowl, mix all ingredients except lamb. Spread mixture on one side of each lamb chop.
2. Place lamb on grill, coated side up, over medium heat. Cover grill; cook 12 to 15 minutes or until thermometer inserted in center reads 145°F.

Nutrition Info:

- 330 cal., 14g fat (5g sat. fat), 140 chol., 880mg sod., 7g carb. (6g sugars, 0g fiber), 43g pro.

Southwest Steak

Servings: 8 | Cooking Time: 25 Minutes

Ingredients:

- 1/4 cup lime juice
- 6 garlic cloves, minced
- 4 teaspoons chili powder
- 4 teaspoons canola oil
- 1 teaspoon salt
- 1 teaspoon crushed red pepper flakes
- 1 teaspoon pepper
- 2 beef flank steaks (1 pound each)

Directions:

1. In a large resealable plastic bag, combine the first seven ingredients; add beef. Seal bag and turn to coat; refrigerate for 4 hours or overnight.
2. Drain and discard marinade. Using long-handled tongs, moisten a paper towel with cooking oil and lightly coat the grill rack. Grill the beef, covered, over medium heat or broil 4 in. from the heat for 5-7 minutes on each side or until meat reaches desired doneness (for medium-rare, a thermometer should read 145°; medium, 160°; well-done, 170°).
3. Let stand for 5 minutes; thinly slice across the grain.

Nutrition Info:

- 187 cal., 10 g fat (4 g sat. fat), 54 mg chol., 259 mg sodium, 2 g carb., trace fiber, 22 g pro.

Prosciutto-pepper Pork Chops

Servings: 4 | Cooking Time: 20 Minutes

Ingredients:

- 4 boneless pork loin chops (4 ounces each)
- 1/8 teaspoon garlic powder
- 1/8 teaspoon pepper
- 2 teaspoons canola oil
- 4 thin slices prosciutto or deli ham
- 1/2 cup julienned roasted sweet red peppers
- 2 slices reduced-fat provolone cheese, cut in half

Directions:

1. Sprinkle pork chops with garlic powder and pepper. In a large nonstick skillet, cook chops in oil over medium heat for 4-5 minutes on each side or until a thermometer reads 145°.
2. Top each pork chop with prosciutto, red peppers and cheese. Cover and cook for 1-2 minutes or until the cheese is melted. Let stand for 5 minutes before serving.

Nutrition Info:

- 237 cal., 12 g fat (4 g sat. fat), 72 mg chol., 483 mg sodium, 1 g carb., trace fiber, 28 g pro.

Steak Marsala

Servings: 4 | Cooking Time: 20 Minutes

Ingredients:

- 4 beef tenderloin steaks, ¾ inch thick (about 1 lb)
- ½ teaspoon salt
- ¼ teaspoon pepper
- 2 cloves garlic, crushed
- 1 tablespoon drained capers
- ½ cup Marsala wine or nonalcoholic red wine

Directions:

1. Sprinkle both sides of each beef steak with salt and pepper. Rub with garlic. Spray 10-inch skillet with cooking spray; heat over medium-high heat. Add beef; cook 6 to 8 minutes, turning once, until desired doneness. Remove beef from skillet; cover to keep warm.
2. Add capers and wine to skillet. Heat to boiling over high heat. Cook uncovered 3 to 4 minutes, stirring frequently, until liquid is slightly reduced. Serve sauce over beef.

Nutrition Info:

- 190 cal., 8g fat (3g sat. fat), 50 chol., 390mg sod., 2g carb. (0g sugars, 0g fiber), 26g pro.

Country-style Ham And Potato Casserole

Servings: 4 | Cooking Time: 15 Minutes

Ingredients:

- 6 ounces lean smoked deli ham, (preferably Virginia ham), thinly sliced and chopped
- 1 pound red potatoes, scrubbed and thinly sliced
- 1 medium onion, thinly sliced
- 1/3 cup shredded, reduced-fat, sharp cheddar cheese

Directions:

1. Preheat the oven to 350°F.
2. Place a medium nonstick skillet over medium-high heat until hot. Coat the skillet with nonstick cooking spray, add ham, and cook 5 minutes or until the ham edges are beginning to lightly brown, stirring frequently. Remove from the heat and set the ham aside on a separate plate.
3. Layer half of the potatoes and half of the onions in the bottom of the skillet. Top with the ham and repeat with layers of potatoes and onions. Sprinkle with black pepper, if desired, and cover tightly with a sheet of foil.
4. Bake 35–40 minutes or until the potatoes are tender when pierced with a fork. Remove from the oven, top with cheese, and let stand, uncovered, for 3 minutes to melt the cheese and develop flavors.

Nutrition Info:

- 170 cal., 2g fat (1g sag. fat), 25mg chol, 420mg sod., 23g carb (4g sugars, 2g fiber), 13g pro.

Homestyle Double-onion Roast

Servings: 6 | Cooking Time:1 Hour And 10 Minutes

Ingredients:

- 1 pound carrots, scrubbed, quartered lengthwise, and cut into 3-inch pieces
- 2 medium onions (8 ounces total), cut in 1/2-inch wedges and separated
- 1 3/4 pounds lean eye of round roast
- 1/4 cup water
- 2 1/2 tablespoons onion soup mix

Directions:

1. Preheat the oven to 325°F.
2. Coat a 13 × 9-inch nonstick baking pan with nonstick cooking spray, arrange the carrots and onions in the pan, and set aside.
3. Place a medium nonstick skillet over medium-high heat until hot. Coat the skillet with nonstick cooking spray, add the beef, and brown 2 minutes. Turn and brown another 2 minutes.
4. Place the beef in the center of the baking pan on top of the vegetables. Add the water to the skillet and scrap up the pan drippings, then pour them over the beef. Sprinkle evenly with the soup mix.
5. Cover the pan tightly with foil and cook 1 hour and 5 minutes or until a meat thermometer reaches 135°F. Place the beef on a cutting board and let stand 15 minutes before slicing. (The temperature will rise another 10°F while the beef stands.)
6. Keep the vegetables in the pan covered to keep warm. Place the beef slices on a serving platter, arrange the vegetables around the beef, and spoon the pan liquids evenly over the beef.

Nutrition Info:

- 220 cal., 4g fat (1g sag. fat), 60mg chol, 410mg sod., 13g carb (5g sugars, 3g fiber), 32g pro.

Chili-stuffed Potatoes

Servings: 4 | Cooking Time:10 Minutes

Ingredients:

- 4 (8-ounce) baking potatoes, preferably Yukon Gold, scrubbed and pierced several times with a fork
- 12 ounces 90% lean ground beef
- 3/4 cup water
- 1 (1.25-ounce) packet chili seasoning mix

Directions:

1. Microwave the potatoes on HIGH 10–11 minutes or until they are tender when pierced with a fork.
2. Meanwhile, place a large nonstick skillet over medium-high heat until hot. Coat the skillet with nonstick cooking spray, add the beef, and cook until the beef is no longer pink, stirring frequently.
3. Add the water and chili seasoning and stir. Cook 1–2 minutes or until thickened.
4. Split the potatoes almost in half and fluff with a fork. Spoon 1/2 cup chili onto each potato and top with sour cream or cheese (if desired).

Nutrition Info:

- 350 cal., 8g fat (2g sag. fat), 50mg chol, 410mg sod., 48g carb (3g sugars, 5g fiber), 21g pro.

Roasted Leg Of Lamb

Servings: 12 | Cooking Time: 120 Minutes

Ingredients:

- 1/3 cup olive oil
- 1/4 cup minced fresh rosemary
- 1/4 cup finely chopped onion
- 4 garlic cloves, minced
- 1/2 teaspoon salt
- 1/4 teaspoon pepper
- 1 bone-in leg of lamb (5 to 6 pounds), trimmed

Directions:

1. Preheat oven to 325°. Combine the oil, rosemary, onion, garlic, salt and pepper; rub over lamb. Place fat side up on a rack in a shallow roasting pan.
2. Bake, uncovered, 2 to 2 1/2 hours or until meat reaches desired doneness (for medium-rare, a thermometer should read 145°; medium, 160°; well-done, 170°), basting occasionally with pan juices. Let stand 15 minutes before slicing.

Nutrition Info:

- 212 cal., 12 g fat (3 g sat. fat), 85 mg chol., 137 mg sodium, 1 g carb., trace fiber, 24 g pro.

Sriracha-roasted Pork With Sweet Potatoes

Servings: 4 | Cooking Time:25 Minutes

Ingredients:

- 1 pound pork tenderloin
- 1 pound sweet potatoes, peeled and cut into 1-inch chunks (1/4 tsp salt and pepper)
- 2 tablespoons honey
- 1 tablespoon hot pepper sauce, such as sriracha

Directions:

1. Preheat oven to 425°F.
2. Heat a large skillet coated with cooking spray over medium-high heat. Add the pork and brown on all sides, about 5 minutes total.
3. Place potatoes in a 13 × 9-inch baking pan. Coat potatoes with cooking spray and toss until well coated. Place the pork in the center of the potatoes and sprinkle 1/4 teaspoon salt and 1/4 teaspoon pepper evenly over all.
4. In a small bowl, combine the honey and sriracha sauce; set aside.
5. Bake 10 minutes, stir potatoes, spoon sauce over pork, and continue baking 15 minutes or until internal temperature of the pork reaches 150°F.
6. Place the pork on a cutting board and let stand 3 minutes before slicing. Meanwhile, gently toss the potatoes in the pan with any pan drippings. Cover to keep warm. Serve with pork.

Nutrition Info:

- 280 cal., 5g fat (1g sag. fat), 75mg chol, 310mg sod., 31g carb (6g sugars, 6g fiber), 26g pro.

Maple Pork With Figs

Servings: 4 | Cooking Time: 25 Minutes

Ingredients:

- 4 bone-in pork loin chops, ½ inch thick (about 1¼ lb), trimmed of fat
- ½ teaspoon salt
- ½ cup apple juice or dry red wine
- ¼ cup real maple syrup
- ⅓ cup coarsely chopped dried figs
- 1 teaspoon cornstarch
- ¼ cup water

Directions:

1. Spray 12-inch skillet with cooking spray; heat skillet over medium-high heat. Sprinkle pork with salt; place in skillet. Cook about 5 minutes, turning once, until browned. Remove from skillet; keep warm.
2. In same skillet, cook apple juice, maple syrup and figs over medium-high heat 5 minutes, stirring frequently.
3. In small bowl, mix cornstarch and water; stir into juice mixture. Cook over medium-high heat about 2 minutes, stirring constantly, until thickened and clear.
4. Reduce heat to medium. Return pork to skillet; spoon sauce over pork. Simmer about 2 minutes or until pork is no longer pink in center.

Nutrition Info:

- 260 cal., 8g fat (2.5g sat. fat), 65 chol., 340mg sod., 26g carb. (21g sugars, 1g fiber), 22g pro.

Sausage Pilaf Peppers

Servings: 4 | Cooking Time:40 Minutes

Ingredients:

- 4 medium green bell peppers
- 6 ounces reduced-fat pork breakfast sausage
- 3/4 cup uncooked instant brown rice
- 2/3 cup salsa, divided use

Directions:

1. Preheat the oven to 350°F.
2. Slice the tops off of each pepper and discard the seeds and membrane, leaving the peppers whole.
3. Coat a large nonstick skillet with nonstick cooking spray and place over medium-high heat until hot. Add the sausage and cook until it's no longer pink, breaking up large pieces while stirring.
4. Remove from the heat and add the rice and all but 1/4 cup salsa. Stir gently to blend.
5. Fill the peppers with equal amounts of the mixture and top each with 1 tablespoon salsa. Place the peppers in the skillet and cover tightly with foil. Bake 35 minutes or until the peppers are tender.

Nutrition Info:

- 260 cal., 8g fat (2g sag. fat), 20mg chol, 450mg sod., 37g carb (5g sugars, 5g fiber), 11g pro.

Simple Teriyaki Steak Dinner

Servings: 4 | Cooking Time: 20 Minutes

Ingredients:

- 1 tablespoon butter or margarine
- 1 medium bell pepper (any color), coarsely chopped (1 cup)
- 1½ cups sliced fresh mushrooms (about 5 oz)
- 4 boneless beef top loin steaks (New York, Kansas City or strip steaks), about ¾ inch thick (6 oz each)
- ½ teaspoon garlic salt
- ¼ teaspoon coarse ground black pepper
- ¼ cup teriyaki baste and glaze (from 12-oz bottle)
- 2 tablespoons water

Directions:

1. In 12-inch nonstick skillet, melt butter over medium-high heat. Add bell pepper; cook 2 minutes, stirring frequently. Stir in mushrooms. Cook 2 to 3 minutes, stirring frequently, until vegetables are tender. Remove vegetable mixture from skillet; cover to keep warm.
2. Sprinkle beef steaks with garlic salt and pepper. In same skillet, cook steaks over medium heat 6 to 8 minutes, turning once or twice, until desired doneness.
3. Return vegetables to skillet. Stir teriyaki glaze and water into vegetables and spoon over steaks. Cook about 1 minute, stirring vegetables occasionally, until thoroughly heated.

Nutrition Info:

- 330 cal., 15g fat (6g sat. fat), 80 chol., 600mg sod., 8g carb. (6g sugars, 0g fiber), 41g pro.

Pork With Caramelized Onions

Servings: 4 | Cooking Time: 25 Minutes

Ingredients:

- 1 lb pork tenderloin
- ½ teaspoon salt
- ¼ teaspoon paprika
- 1 large onion, thinly sliced (2 cups)
- ¼ teaspoon sugar

Directions:

1. Cut pork into ½-inch slices. Sprinkle both sides of pork with salt and paprika.
2. Heat 10-inch nonstick skillet over medium-high heat. Add pork; cook 6 to 8 minutes, turning once, until no longer pink in center. Remove pork from skillet; keep warm. Wipe out skillet.
3. Heat same skillet over medium-high heat. Add onion; cook 1 minute, stirring frequently. Reduce heat to medium. Stir in sugar. Cook about 3 minutes longer, stirring frequently, until onion is soft and golden brown. Spoon over pork.

Nutrition Info:

- 170 cal., 4.5g fat (1.5g sat. fat), 70 chol., 350mg sod., 6g carb. (3g sugars, 1g fiber), 26g pro.

Cheesy Steak And Potato Skillet

Servings: 4 | Cooking Time: 30 Minutes

Ingredients:

- 1 lb boneless beef sirloin steak, cut into 4 serving pieces
- ½ teaspoon garlic-pepper blend
- ¼ teaspoon seasoned salt
- 1 tablespoon canola oil
- 1½ cups frozen bell pepper and onion stir-fry (from 1-lb bag)
- 1 bag (1 lb 4 oz) refrigerated home-style potato slices
- ¾ cup shredded reduced-fat sharp Cheddar cheese (3 oz)

Directions:

1. Sprinkle beef pieces with ¼ teaspoon of the garlic-pepper blend and ⅛ teaspoon of the seasoned salt. In 12-inch nonstick skillet, cook beef over medium-high heat 3 to 4 minutes, turning once or twice, until brown and desired doneness. Remove from skillet; keep warm.
2. In same skillet, heat oil over medium heat. Add stir-fry vegetables; cook 2 minutes, stirring frequently. Add potatoes; sprinkle with remaining ¼ teaspoon garlic-pepper blend and ⅛ teaspoon seasoned salt. Cook uncovered 8 to 10 minutes, stirring frequently, until tender.
3. Place beef in skillet with potatoes, pushing potatoes around beef. Cook 1 to 2 minutes, turning beef once, until thoroughly heated. Sprinkle with cheese; cover and heat until cheese is melted.

Nutrition Info:

- 350 cal., 9g fat (2.5g sat. fat), 70 chol., 510mg sod., 33g carb. (3g sugars, 2g fiber), 34g pro.

Smoky Sirloin

Servings: 4 | Cooking Time:12 Minutes

Ingredients:

- 1 pound boneless sirloin steak, about 3/4-inch thick
- 1 1/2 teaspoons smoked paprika
- 2 tablespoons Worcestershire sauce
- 2 tablespoons balsamic vinegar

Directions:

1. Sprinkle both sides of the beef with paprika, 1/4 teaspoon salt, and 1/4 teaspoon pepper. Press down lightly to adhere. Let stand 15 minutes at room temperature.
2. Heat a large skillet coated with cooking spray over medium-high heat. Cook beef 4 to 5 minutes on each side. Place on cutting board and let stand 5 minutes before slicing.
3. Combine 1/4 cup water, Worcestershire sauce, and vinegar. Pour into the skillet with any pan residue and bring to a boil over medium-high heat. Boil 2 minutes or until reduced to 2 tablespoons liquid. Pour over sliced beef.

Nutrition Info:

- 150 cal., 3g fat (1g sag. fat), 70mg chol, 280mg sod., 3g carb (2g sugars, 0g fiber), 26g pro.

Grapefruit-zested Pork

Servings: 4 | Cooking Time:6 Minutes

Ingredients:

- 3 tablespoons lite soy sauce
- 1/2–1 teaspoon grapefruit zest
- 3 tablespoons grapefruit juice
- 1 jalapeño pepper, seeded and finely chopped, or 1/8–1/4 teaspoon dried red pepper flakes
- 4 thin lean pork chops with bone in (about 1 1/4 pounds total)

Directions:

1. Combine all ingredients in a large zippered plastic bag. Seal tightly and toss back and forth to coat evenly. Refrigerate overnight or at least 8 hours.
2. Preheat the broiler.
3. Coat the broiler rack and pan with nonstick cooking spray, arrange the pork chops on the rack (discarding the marinade), and broil 2 inches away from the heat source for 3 minutes. Turn and broil 3 minutes longer or until the pork is no longer pink in the center.

Nutrition Info:

- 130 cal., 3g fat (1g sag. fat), 60mg chol, 270mg sod., 2g carb (1g sugars, 0g fiber), 23g pro.

Sweet Sherry'd Pork Tenderloin

Servings: 4 | Cooking Time:22 Minutes

Ingredients:

- 1 pound pork tenderloin
- 1/4 cup dry sherry (divided use)
- 3 tablespoons lite soy sauce (divided use)
- 1/3 cup peach all-fruit spread

Directions:

1. Place the pork, 2 tablespoons sherry, and 2 tablespoons soy sauce in a quart-sized zippered plastic bag. Seal tightly and toss back and forth to coat evenly. Refrigerate overnight or at least 8 hours.
2. Stir the fruit spread, 2 tablespoons sherry, and 1 tablespoon soy sauce together in a small bowl. Cover with plastic wrap and refrigerate until needed.
3. Preheat the oven to 425°F.
4. Remove the pork from the marinade and discard the marinade. Place a medium nonstick skillet over medium-high heat until hot. Coat the skillet with nonstick cooking spray, add the pork, and brown on all sides.
5. Place the pork in a 9-inch pie pan and bake 15 minutes or until the pork is barely pink in the center. Place the pork on a cutting board and let stand 3 minutes before slicing.
6. Meanwhile, place the fruit spread mixture in the skillet and bring to a boil over medium-high heat, stirring frequently. Place the sauce on the bottom of a serving plate and arrange the pork on top. Sprinkle evenly with black pepper, if desired.

Nutrition Info:

- 190 cal., 3g fat (1g sag. fat), 60mg chol, 320mg sod., 14g carb (11g sugars, 0g fiber), 23g pro.

Fish & Seafood Recipes

Oven-roasted Salmon

Servings:4 | Cooking Time:10 Minutes

Ingredients:

- 1 (1½-pound) skin-on salmon fillet, 1 inch thick
- 1 teaspoon extra-virgin olive oil
- ¼ teaspoon salt
- ⅛ teaspoon pepper

Directions:

1. Adjust oven rack to lowest position, place aluminum foil–lined rimmed baking sheet on rack, and heat oven to 500 degrees. Cut salmon crosswise into 4 fillets, then make 4 or 5 shallow slashes about an inch apart along skin side of each piece, being careful not to cut into flesh. Pat fillets dry with paper towels, rub with oil, and sprinkle with salt and pepper.
2. Once oven reaches 500 degrees, reduce oven temperature to 275 degrees. Remove sheet from oven and carefully place salmon, skin-side down, on hot sheet. Roast until centers are still translucent when checked with tip of paring knife and register 125 degrees (for medium-rare), 4 to 6 minutes.
3. Slide spatula along underside of fillets and transfer to individual serving plates or serving platter, leaving skin behind; discard skin. Serve.

Nutrition Info:

- 360 cal., 24g fat (5g sag. fat), 95mg chol, 250mg sod., 0g carb (0g sugars, 0g fiber), 35g pro.

Pesto Grilled Salmon

Servings:12 | Cooking Time: 30 Minutes

Ingredients:

- 1 salmon fillet (3 pounds)
- 1/2 cup prepared pesto
- 2 green onions, finely chopped
- 1/4 cup lemon juice
- 2 garlic cloves, minced

Directions:

1. Moisten a paper towel with cooking oil; using long-handled tongs, lightly coat the grill rack. Place salmon skin side down on grill rack. Grill, covered, over medium heat or broil 4 in. from the heat for 5 minutes.
2. In a small bowl, combine the pesto, onions, lemon juice and garlic. Carefully spoon some of the pesto mixture over salmon. Grill for about15-20 minutes longer or until the fish flakes easily with a fork, basting occasionally with the remaining pesto mixture.

Nutrition Info:

- 262 cal., 17g fat (4g sat. fat), 70mg chol., 147mg sod., 1g carb. (0 sugars, 0 fiber), 25g pro.

Salmon With Lemon-dill Butter

Servings: 2 | Cooking Time: 15 Minutes

Ingredients:

- 2 salmon fillets (4 ounces each)
- 5 teaspoons reduced-fat butter, melted
- 3/4 teaspoon lemon juice
- 1/2 teaspoon grated lemon peel
- 1/2 teaspoon snipped fresh dill

Directions:

1. Place salmon skin side down on a broiler pan. Combine the butter, lemon juice, lemon peel and dill. Brush one-third of mixture over salmon. Broil 3-4 in. from the heat for 7-9 minutes or until fish flakes easily with a fork, basting occasionally with remaining butter mixture.

Nutrition Info:

- 219 cal., 15 g fat (5 g sat. fat), 69 mg chol., 136 mg sodium, 1 g carb., trace fiber, 19 g pro.

Parmesan Fish Fillets

Servings: 2 | Cooking Time: 30 Minutes

Ingredients:

- 1/4 cup egg substitute
- 1 tablespoon fat-free milk
- 1/3 cup grated Parmesan cheese
- 2 tablespoons all-purpose flour
- 2 tilapia fillets (5 ounces each)

Directions:

1. In a shallow bowl, combine egg substitute and milk. In another shallow bowl, combine cheese and flour. Dip fillets in egg mixture, then coat with cheese mixture.
2. Place on a baking sheet coated with cooking spray. Bake at 350° for 20-25 minutes or until the fish flakes easily with a fork.

Nutrition Info:

- 196 cal., 5 g fat (3 g sat. fat), 78 mg chol., 279 mg sodium, 5 g carb., trace fiber, 33 g pro.

No-fry Fish Fry

Servings: 4 | Cooking Time:6 Minutes

Ingredients:

- 2 tablespoons yellow cornmeal
- 2 teaspoons Cajun seasoning
- 4 (4-ounce) tilapia filets (or any mild, lean white fish filets), rinsed and patted dry
- 1/8 teaspoon salt
- Lemon wedges (optional)

Directions:

1. Preheat the broiler.
2. Coat a broiler rack and pan with nonstick cooking spray and set aside.
3. Mix the cornmeal and Cajun seasoning thoroughly in a shallow pan, such as a pie plate. Coat each filet with nonstick cooking spray and coat evenly with the cornmeal mixture.
4. Place the filets on the rack and broil 6 inches away from the heat source for 3 minutes on each side.
5. Place the filets on a serving platter, sprinkle each evenly with salt, and serve with lemon wedges, if desired.

Nutrition Info:

- 130 cal., 2g fat (0g sag. fat), 50mg chol, 250mg sod., 4g carb (0g sugars, 0g fiber), 23g pro.

Pan-seared Sesame-crusted Tuna Steaks

Servings:4 | Cooking Time:8 Minutes

Ingredients:

- ¾ cup sesame seeds
- 4 (6-ounce) skinless tuna steaks, 1 inch thick
- 2 tablespoons canola oil
- ¼ teaspoon salt
- ⅛ teaspoon pepper

Directions:

1. Spread sesame seeds in shallow baking dish. Pat tuna steaks dry with paper towels, rub steaks all over with 1 tablespoon oil, then sprinkle with salt and pepper. Press both sides of each steak in sesame seeds to coat.
2. Heat remaining 1 tablespoon oil in 12-inch nonstick skillet over medium-high heat until just smoking. Place steaks in skillet and cook until seeds are golden and tuna is translucent red at center when checked with tip of paring knife and registers 110 degrees (for rare), 1 to 2 minutes per side. Transfer tuna to cutting board and slice ½ inch thick. Serve.

Nutrition Info:

- 330 cal., 15g fat (1g sag. fat), 65mg chol, 250mg sod., 2g carb (0g sugars, 1g fiber), 45g pro.

Lemon-pepper Halibut And Squash Packets

Servings: 4 | Cooking Time: 30 Minutes

Ingredients:

- 1 lb halibut fillets (½ to ¾ inch thick)
- 2 teaspoons dried basil leaves
- 1 teaspoon lemon-pepper seasoning
- 1 teaspoon seasoned salt
- 3 medium zucchini or yellow summer squash, cut into 2 × 1-inch strips
- 1 medium red bell pepper, cut into 1-inch pieces
- 2 tablespoons olive or canola oil

Directions:

1. Heat gas or charcoal grill. Cut 4 (18 × 12-inch) sheets of heavy-duty foil; spray with cooking spray. Cut halibut into 4 serving pieces if necessary. Place 1 fish piece on center of each sheet. Sprinkle fillets with 1 teaspoon of the basil, ½ teaspoon of the lemon-pepper seasoning and ½ teaspoon of the seasoned salt. Arrange zucchini and bell pepper evenly over fish. Sprinkle with remaining basil, lemon-pepper seasoning and seasoned salt. Drizzle with oil.
2. Bring up 2 sides of foil over fish and vegetables so edges meet. Seal edges, making tight ½-inch fold; fold again, allowing space for heat circulation and expansion. Fold other sides to seal.
3. Place packets on grill over medium heat. Cover grill; cook 15 to 20 minutes, rotating packets ½ turn after 8 minutes, until fish flakes easily with fork and vegetables are tender. To serve, cut large X across top of each packet; carefully fold back foil to allow steam to escape.

Nutrition Info:

- 200 cal., 9g fat (1.5g sat. fat), 60 chol., 540mg sod., 7g carb. (4g sugars, 2g fiber), 24g pro.

Buttery Lemon Grilled Fish On Grilled Asparagus

Servings: 4 | Cooking Time:12 Minutes

Ingredients:

- 1 pound asparagus spears, ends trimmed
- 4 (4-ounce) cod filets, rinsed and patted dry
- Juice and zest of a medium lemon
- 1/4 cup light butter with canola oil

Directions:

1. Heat a grill or grill pan over medium-high heat. Coat the asparagus with cooking spray and cook 6–8 minutes or until just tender-crisp, turning occasionally. Set aside on a rimmed serving platter and cover to keep warm.
2. Coat both sides of the fish with cooking spray, sprinkle with 1/4 teaspoon black pepper, if desired, and cook 3 minutes on each side or until opaque in center.
3. Meanwhile, combine the light butter, lemon zest and 1/4 teaspoon salt, if desired, in a small bowl.
4. Spoon the butter mixture over the asparagus and spread over all. Top with the fish and squeeze lemon juice over fish.

Nutrition Info:

- 160 cal., 6g fat (1g sag. fat), 50mg chol, 210mg sod., 6g carb (3g sugars, 3g fiber), 23g pro.

Baked Italian Tilapia

Servings: 4 | Cooking Time: 50 Minutes

Ingredients:

- 4 tilapia fillets (6 ounces each)
- 1/4 teaspoon pepper
- 1 can (14 1/2 ounces) diced tomatoes with basil, oregano and garlic, drained
- 1 large onion, halved and thinly sliced
- 1 medium green pepper, julienned
- 1/4 cup shredded Parmesan cheese

Directions:

1. Place tilapia in a 13-in. x 9-in. baking dish coated with cooking spray; sprinkle with pepper. Spoon the tomatoes over tilapia; top with onion and green pepper.
2. Cover and bake at 350° for 30 minutes. Uncover; sprinkle with cheese. Bake 10-15 minutes longer or until fish flakes easily with a fork.

Nutrition Info:

- 215 cal., 4 g fat (2 g sat. fat), 86 mg chol., 645 mg sodium, 12 g carb., 2 g fiber, 36 g pro.

Shrimp And Noodles Parmesan

Servings: 4 | Cooking Time:10 Minutes

Ingredients:

- 8 ounces uncooked whole-wheat no-yolk egg noodles
- 1 pound peeled raw shrimp, rinsed and patted dry
- 1/4 cup no-trans-fat margarine (35% vegetable oil)
- 1/4 teaspoon salt
- 3 tablespoons grated fresh Parmesan cheese

Directions:

1. Cook noodles according to package directions, omitting any salt or fat.
2. Meanwhile, place a large nonstick skillet over medium heat until hot. Coat with nonstick cooking spray and sauté the shrimp for 4–5 minutes or until opaque in the center, stirring frequently.
3. Drain the noodles well in a colander and place in a pasta bowl. Add the margarine, shrimp, salt, and black pepper, to taste (if desired), and toss gently. Sprinkle evenly with the Parmesan cheese.

Nutrition Info:

- 340 cal., 7g fat (1g sag. fat), 190mg chol, 410mg sod., 42g carb (0g sugars, 6g fiber), 33g pro.

Two-sauce Cajun Fish

Servings: 4 | Cooking Time:12–15 Minutes

Ingredients:

- 4 (4-ounce) tilapia filets (or any mild, lean white fish filets), rinsed and patted dry
- 1/2 teaspoon seafood seasoning
- 1 (14.5-ounce) can stewed tomatoes with Cajun seasonings, well drained
- 2 tablespoons no-trans-fat margarine (35% vegetable oil)

Directions:

1. Preheat the oven to 400°F.
2. Coat a broiler rack and pan with nonstick cooking spray, arrange the fish filets on the rack about 2 inches apart, and sprinkle them evenly with the seafood seasoning.
3. Place the tomatoes in a blender and puree until just smooth. Set aside 1/4 cup of the mixture in a small glass bowl.
4. Spoon the remaining tomatoes evenly over the top of each filet and bake 12–15 minutes or until the filets are opaque in the center.
5. Meanwhile, add the margarine to the reserved 1/4 cup tomato mixture and microwave on HIGH 20 seconds or until the mixture is just melted. Stir to blend well.
6. Place the filets on a serving platter, spoon the tomato-margarine mixture over the center of each filet, and sprinkle each lightly with chopped fresh parsley, if desired.

Nutrition Info:

- 150 cal., 5g fat (1g sag. fat), 50mg chol, 250mg sod., 4g carb (3g sugars, 1g fiber), 23g pro.

Italian-style Tilapia Fillets

Servings: 4 | Cooking Time: 15 Minutes

Ingredients:

- 1 lb tilapia or catfish fillets, cut into 4 serving pieces
- 1 teaspoon salt-free seasoning blend
- 1 tablespoon olive or canola oil
- 1 clove garlic, finely chopped
- 1 pint (2 cups) cherry tomatoes, cut in half
- ¼ cup sliced ripe olives, drained

Directions:

1. Sprinkle both sides of fish fillets with seasoning blend. In 12-inch nonstick skillet, heat oil over medium-high heat. Add fish; cook 6 to 8 minutes, turning once, until golden. Remove fish from skillet; cover to keep warm.
2. Heat same skillet over medium-high heat. Add garlic; cook and stir 30 seconds. Add tomatoes; cook about 3 minutes, stirring occasionally, until softened and juicy. Stir in olives. Serve over fish.

Nutrition Info:

- 160 cal., 6g fat (1g sat. fat), 60 chol., 170mg sod., 4g carb. (2g sugars, 1g fiber), 22g pro.

Grilled Salmon Packets

Servings: 4 | Cooking Time: 25 Minutes

Ingredients:

- 4 salmon fillets (6 ounces each)
- 3 cups fresh sugar snap peas
- 1 small sweet red pepper, cut into strips
- 1 small sweet yellow pepper, cut into strips
- 1/4 cup reduced-fat Asian toasted sesame salad dressing

Directions:

1. Place each salmon fillet on a double thickness of heavy-duty foil (about 12 in. square). Combine sugar snap peas and peppers; spoon over salmon. Drizzle with salad dressing. Fold foil around mixture and seal tightly.
2. Grill, covered, over medium heat for 15-20 minutes or until fish flakes easily with a fork. Open foil carefully to allow steam to escape.

Nutrition Info:

- 350 cal., 17 g fat (3 g sat. fat), 85 mg chol., 237 mg sodium, 14 g carb., 4 g fiber, 34 g pro.

Salads Recipes

Salads Recipes

Pear And Bleu Cheese Greens

Servings: 4 | Cooking Time: 4 Minutes

Ingredients:

- 6 cups spring greens
- 1 1/3 cups firm pear slices or green apple slices
- 6 tablespoons fat-free raspberry vinaigrette
- 3 tablespoons crumbled reduced-fat bleu cheese

Directions:

1. Place 1 1/2 cups of the greens on each of 4 salad plates. Arrange 1/3 cup pear slices on each serving.
2. Top with 1 1/2 tablespoons dressing and 3/4 tablespoon of the cheese. Serve immediately.

Nutrition Info:

- 80 cal., 1g fat (0g sag. fat), 5mg chol, 230mg sod., 15g carb (11g sugars, 2g fiber), 2g pro.

Bacon Onion Potato Salad

Servings: 4 | Cooking Time:4 Minutes

Ingredients:

- 12 ounces unpeeled red potatoes, diced (about 3 cups)
- 3 tablespoons reduced-fat ranch salad dressing
- 1/2 cup finely chopped green onion
- 2 tablespoons real bacon bits (not imitation)

Directions:

1. Bring water to boil in a medium saucepan over high heat. Add the potatoes and return to a boil. Reduce the heat, cover tightly, and cook 4 minutes or until just tender when pierced with a fork.
2. Drain the potatoes in a colander and run under cold water until cool, about 30 seconds. Drain well and place in a medium bowl with the remaining ingredients. Toss gently to blend well.
3. Serve immediately or cover with plastic wrap and refrigerate 2 hours for a more blended flavor. To serve, add salt, if desired and toss.

Nutrition Info:

- 110 cal., 3g fat (0g sag. fat), 5mg chol, 250mg sod., 16g carb (2g sugars, 2g fiber), 4g pro.

Crispy Crunch Coleslaw

Servings: 4 | Cooking Time: 7 Minutes

Ingredients:

- 3 cups shredded cabbage mix with carrots and red cabbage
- 1 medium green bell pepper, finely chopped
- 2–3 tablespoons apple cider vinegar
- 2 tablespoons Splenda
- 1/8 teaspoon salt

Directions:

1. Place all ingredients in a large zippered plastic bag, seal tightly, and shake to blend thoroughly.
2. Refrigerate 3 hours before serving to blend flavors. This salad tastes best served the same day you make it.

Nutrition Info:

- 20 cal., 0g fat (0g sag. fat), 0mg chol, 85mg sod., 4g carb (2g sugars, 2g fiber), 0g pro.

Cumin'd Salsa Salad

Servings: 4 | Cooking Time: 3 Minutes

Ingredients:

- 3/4 cup mild or medium salsa fresca (pico de gallo)
- 2 tablespoons water
- 1/4 teaspoon ground cumin
- 8 cups shredded lettuce
- 20 baked bite-sized multi-grain tortilla chips, coarsely crumbled (1 ounce)

Directions:

1. Stir the salsa, water, and cumin together in a small bowl.
2. Place 2 cups of lettuce on each of 4 salad plates, spoon 3 tablespoons picante mixture over each salad, and top with chips.

Nutrition Info:

- 60 cal., 2g fat (0g sag. fat), 0mg chol, 40mg sod., 9g carb (3g sugars, 2g fiber), 2g pro.

Minted Carrot Salad

Servings: 4 | Cooking Time:1 Minute

Ingredients:

- 3 cups thinly sliced carrots (about 12 ounces total)
- 1 tablespoon extra-virgin olive oil
- 1 tablespoon cider vinegar
- 1/3 cup chopped fresh mint (or basil)

Directions:

1. Bring 4 cups water to a rolling boil in a large saucepan. Add the carrots, return to a rolling boil, and cook 30 seconds. Immediately drain in a colander and run under cold water to cool completely. Drain well.
2. Place carrots in a shallow bowl. Top with remaining ingredients and sprinkle evenly with 1/4 teaspoon salt and 1/4 teaspoon pepper. Serve immediately or cover and refrigerate up to 1 hour before serving.

Nutrition Info:

- 75 cal., 4g fat (0g sag. fat), 0mg chol, 70mg sod., 10g carb (5g sugars, 4g fiber), 1g pro.

Tangy Sweet Carrot Pepper Salad

Servings: 4 | Cooking Time:1 Minute

Ingredients:

- 1 1/2 cups peeled sliced carrots (about 1/8-inch thick)
- 2 tablespoons water
- 3/4 cup thinly sliced green bell pepper
- 1/3 cup thinly sliced onion
- 1/4 cup reduced-fat Catalina dressing

Directions:

1. Place carrots and water in a shallow, microwave-safe dish, such as a glass pie plate. Cover with plastic wrap and microwave on HIGH for 1 minute or until carrots are just tender-crisp. Be careful not to overcook them—the carrots should retain some crispness.
2. Immediately place the carrots in a colander and run under cold water about 30 seconds to cool. Shake to drain and place the carrots on paper towels to dry further. Dry the dish.
3. When the carrots are completely cool, return them to the dish, add the remaining ingredients, and toss gently to coat.
4. Serve immediately, or chill 30 minutes for a more blended flavor. Flavors are at their peak if you serve this salad within 30 minutes of adding dressing.

Nutrition Info:

- 60 cal., 0g fat (0g sag. fat), 0mg chol, 200mg sod., 11g carb (7g sugars, 2g fiber), 1g pro.

Carrot Cranberry Matchstick Salad

Servings: 4 | Cooking Time: 5 Minutes

Ingredients:
- 3 cups matchstick carrots
- 1 poblano chili pepper, chopped
- 1/3 cup dried cranberries
- Zest and juice of 1 medium lemon

Directions:
1. Combine the ingredients with 1/8 teaspoon salt in a large bowl. Cover and refrigerate 1 hour before serving.

Nutrition Info:
- 70 cal., 0g fat (0g sag. fat), 0mg chol, 105mg sod., 19g carb (11g sugars, 4g fiber), 1g pro.

Zesty Citrus Melon

Servings: 4 | Cooking Time: 5 Minutes

Ingredients:
- 1/4 cup orange juice
- 2–3 tablespoons lemon juice
- 1 teaspoon honey
- 3 cups diced honeydew or cantaloupe melon

Directions:
1. Stir the orange juice, lemon zest (if using), lemon juice, and honey together in a small bowl.
2. Place the melon on a serving plate and pour the juice mixture evenly over all. For peak flavor, serve within 1 hour.

Nutrition Info:
- 60 cal., 0g fat (0g sag. fat), 0mg chol, 25mg sod., 15g carb (13g sugars, 1g fiber), 1g pro.

Pork And Avocado Salad

Servings: 4 | Cooking Time:10 Minutes

Ingredients:
- 1 pound boneless center-cut pork loin chops
- 2 ripe medium avocados, chopped
- 1/4 cup fresh lemon
- 1 cup chopped fresh parsley or cilantro

Directions:
1. Heat a grill pan or large skillet coated with cooking spray over medium-high heat. Cook the pork 4 minutes on each side or until slightly pink in center. Place on cutting board to cool.
2. Chop pork and place in a large bowl with 1/2 teaspoon salt and 1/2 teaspoon pepper, if desired, and remaining ingredients; toss gently until well blended.

Nutrition Info:
- 260 cal., 13g fat (2g sag. fat), 70mg chol, 85mg sod., 8g carb (1g sugars, 5g fiber), 28g pro.

Chicken Kale Salad With Fresh Ginger Dressing

Servings: 4 | Cooking Time:12 Minutes

Ingredients:

- 1 pound boneless, skinless chicken breast
- 8 cups packed spinach with baby kale greens
- 3/4 cup light raspberry salad dressing, such as Newman's Own
- 2 to 3 teaspoons grated gingerroot

Directions:

1. Heat a grill or grill pan over medium-high heat. Coat the chicken with cooking spray, sprinkle with 1/4 teaspoon salt and 1/4 teaspoon pepper, if desired. Cook 6 minutes on each side or until no longer pink in center. Let cool and thinly slice.
2. Place equal amounts of the greens and chicken on four dinner plates. Whisk together the salad dressing and ginger until well blended. Spoon equal amounts over all.

Nutrition Info:

- 230 cal., 10g fat (1g sag. fat), 85mg chol, 440mg sod., 6g carb (3g sugars, 2g fiber), 28g pro.

Ginger'd Ambrosia

Servings: 4 | Cooking Time:5–10 Minutes

Ingredients:

- 3 medium navel oranges, peeled and cut into bite-sized sections (about 1 1/2 cups total)
- 3 tablespoons flaked, sweetened, shredded coconut
- 2–3 teaspoons grated gingerroot
- 4 fresh or canned pineapple slices, packed in juice, drained

Directions:

1. Place all ingredients except the pineapple in a medium bowl and toss gently. If desired, add 1 teaspoon pourable sugar substitute. Let stand 5–10 minutes to develop flavors.
2. Arrange each pineapple slice on a salad plate and spoon a rounded 1/3 cup of the orange mixture on each slice.

Nutrition Info:

- 80 cal., 1g fat (1g sag. fat), 0mg chol, 10mg sod., 18g carb (14g sugars, 3g fiber), 1g pro.

Mesclun Salad With Goat Cheese And Almonds

Servings:4 | Cooking Time:8minutes

Ingredients:

- 5 ounces (5 cups) mesclun
- 3 tablespoons toasted sliced almonds
- 1 recipe Classic Vinaigrette (this page)
- 2 ounces goat cheese, crumbled (½ cup)

Directions:

1. Gently toss mesclun with almonds and vinaigrette in bowl until well coated. Sprinkle with goat cheese. Serve.

Nutrition Info:

- 170 cal., 16g fat (4g sag. fat), 5mg chol, 160mg sod., 1g carb (0g sugars, 1g fiber), 4g pro.

Caesar'd Chicken Salad

Servings: 4 | Cooking Time: 5 Minutes

Ingredients:

- 1/4 cup fat-free mayonnaise
- 3 tablespoons fat-free Caesar salad dressing
- 2 1/2 cups cooked diced chicken breast
- 1/2 cup finely chopped green onion (green and white parts)

Directions:

1. Stir the mayonnaise and salad dressing together in a medium bowl. Add the chicken, onions, and black pepper, if desired, and stir until well coated.
2. Cover with plastic wrap and refrigerate at least 2 hours to allow flavors to blend. You may refrigerate this salad up to 24 hours before serving.

Nutrition Info:

- 170 cal., 3g fat (1g sag. fat), 75mg chol, 460mg sod., 4g carb (2g sugars, 1g fiber), 28g pro.

Artichoke Tomato Toss

Servings: 4 | Cooking Time: 4 Minutes

Ingredients:

- 1/2 of a 14-ounce can quartered artichoke hearts, drained
- 1 cup grape tomatoes, halved
- 1 tablespoons fat-free Caesar or Italian dressing
- 1 ounce crumbled, reduced-fat, sun-dried tomato and basil feta cheese
- 2 tablespoons chopped fresh parsley (optional)

Directions:

1. In a medium bowl, toss the artichoke hearts, tomatoes, and dressing gently, yet thoroughly. Add the feta and toss gently again.
2. Serve immediately or cover with plastic wrap and refrigerate up to 3 days.

Nutrition Info:

- 45 cal., 1g fat (0g sag. fat), 5mg chol, 270mg sod., 6g carb (2g sugars, 3g fiber), 3g pro.

Lemony Asparagus Spear Salad

Servings: 4 | Cooking Time:1 Minute

Ingredients:

- 1 pound asparagus spears, trimmed
- 1 tablespoon basil pesto sauce
- 2 teaspoons lemon juice
- 1/4 teaspoon salt

Directions:

1. Cover asparagus with water in a large skillet and bring to a boil, then cover tightly and cook 1 minute or until tender-crisp.
2. Immediately drain the asparagus in a colander and run under cold water to cool. Place the asparagus on paper towels to drain, then place on a serving platter.
3. Top the asparagus with the pesto and roll the spears back and forth to coat completely. Drizzle with lemon juice and sprinkle with salt. Flavors are at their peak if you serve this within 30 minutes.

Nutrition Info:

- 25 cal., 1g fat (0g sag. fat), 0mg chol, 190mg sod., 3g carb (1g sugars, 1g fiber), 2g pro.

Roasted Asparagus And Strawberry Salad

Servings: 4 | Cooking Time: 30 Minutes

Ingredients:

- 1 lb fresh asparagus spears
- Cooking spray
- 4 cups torn mixed salad greens
- 1 cup sliced fresh strawberries
- 2 tablespoons chopped pecans
- ¼ cup balsamic vinaigrette dressing
- Cracked black pepper, if desired

Directions:

1. Heat oven to 400°F. Line 15 × 10 × 1-inch pan with foil; spray with cooking spray. Break off tough ends of asparagus as far down as stalks snap easily. Wash asparagus; cut into 1-inch pieces. Place asparagus in single layer in pan; spray with cooking spray.
2. Bake 10 to 12 minutes or until crisp-tender. Cool completely, about 10 minutes.
3. In medium bowl, mix greens, asparagus, strawberries, pecans and dressing. Sprinkle with pepper.

Nutrition Info:

- 120 cal., 8g fat (0.5g sat. fat), 0 chol., 170mg sod., 10g carb. (6g sugars, 3g fiber), 3g pro.

Balsamic Bean Salsa Salad

Servings: 4 | Cooking Time: 15 Minutes

Ingredients:
- 15-ounce can black beans, rinsed and drained
- 1/2 cup chopped red bell pepper
- 1/4 cup finely chopped red onion
- 2 tablespoons balsamic vinegar

Directions:
1. Toss all ingredients in a medium bowl.
2. Let stand 15 minutes to develop flavors.

Nutrition Info:
- 100 cal., 0g fat (0g sag. fat), 0mg chol, 80mg sod., 18g carb (4g sugars, 6g fiber), 6g pro.

Lemon Vinaigrette

Servings:1 | Cooking Time:x

Ingredients:
- This vinaigrette is best for dressing mild greens.
- ¼ teaspoon grated lemon zest plus 1 tablespoon juice
- ½ teaspoon mayonnaise
- ½ teaspoon Dijon mustard
- ⅛ teaspoon salt
- Pinch pepper
- 3 tablespoons extra-virgin olive oil

Directions:

1. Whisk lemon zest and juice, mayonnaise, mustard, salt, and pepper together in bowl. While whisking constantly, drizzle in oil until completely emulsified. (Vinaigrette can be refrigerated for up to 1 week; whisk to recombine.)

Nutrition Info:
- 100 cal., 11g fat (1g sag. fat), 0mg chol, 90mg sod., 0g carb (0g sugars, 0g fiber), 0g pro.

Sausage Spinach Salad

Servings: 2 | Cooking Time: 20 Minutes

Ingredients:

- 4 teaspoons olive oil, divided
- 2 fully cooked Italian chicken sausage links (3 ounces each), cut into 1/4-inch slices
- 1/2 medium onion, halved and sliced
- 4 cups fresh baby spinach
- 1 1/2 teaspoons balsamic vinegar
- 1 teaspoon stone-ground mustard

Directions:

1. In a large nonstick skillet coated with cooking spray, heat 1 teaspoon oil over medium heat. Add the sausage and onion; cook and stir until sausage is lightly browned and the onion is crisp-tender.
2. Place spinach in a large bowl. In a small bowl, whisk vinegar, mustard and remaining oil. Drizzle over spinach; toss to coat. Add sausage mixture; serve immediately.

Nutrition Info:

- 244 cal., 16 g fat (3 g sat. fat), 65 mg chol., 581 mg sodium, 8 g carb., 2 g fiber, 17 g pro.

Feta'd Tuna With Greens

Servings: 4 | Cooking Time: 6 Minutes

Ingredients:

- 6 cups torn Boston Bibb lettuce, red leaf lettuce, or spring greens
- 3 tablespoons fat-free Caesar salad dressing
- 2 ounces crumbled, reduced-fat, sun-dried tomato and basil feta cheese
- 1 (6.4-ounce) packet tuna, broken in large chunks

Directions:

1. Place the lettuce and salad dressing in a large bowl and toss gently, yet thoroughly, to coat completely.
2. Place 1 1/2 cups of lettuce on each of 4 salad plates. Sprinkle each salad with 1 tablespoon feta and lightly flake equal amounts of tuna in the center of each serving. If desired, add a small amount of dressing (such as fat-free Caesar) to the lettuce.

Nutrition Info:

- 80 cal., 2g fat (1g sag. fat), 25mg chol, 360mg sod., 3g carb (1g sugars, 2g fiber), 15g pro.

Vegetarian Recipes

Frozen Peach Yogurt

Servings: 6 | Cooking Time: 20 Minutes

Ingredients:
- 4 medium peaches, peeled and sliced
- 1 envelope unflavored gelatin
- 1 cup fat-free milk
- 1/2 cup sugar
- Dash salt
- 2 1/2 cups vanilla yogurt
- 2 teaspoons vanilla extract

Directions:

1. Place peaches in a blender. Cover and process until blended; set aside. In a small saucepan, sprinkle gelatin over milk; let stand for 1 minute. Heat over low heat, stirring until the gelatin is completely dissolved. Remove from the heat; stir in sugar and salt until sugar dissolves. Add the yogurt, vanilla and reserved peaches.
2. Fill cylinder of ice cream freezer two-thirds full; freeze according to the manufacturer's directions. When yogurt is frozen, transfer to a freezer container; freeze for 2-4 hours before serving.

Nutrition Info:
- 149 cal., 1 g fat (1 g sat. fat), 4 mg chol., 83 mg sodium, 29 g carb., 1 g fiber, 6 g pro.

Open-faced Grilled Pepper-goat Cheese Sandwiches

Servings: 4 | Cooking Time:25 Minutes

Ingredients:
- 3 large red bell peppers, halved lengthwise
- 1 1/2 tablespoons balsamic vinegar
- 8 ounces whole grain loaf bread, cut in half lengthwise
- 2 ounces crumbled goat cheese

Directions:

1. Heat grill or grill pan over medium-high heat. Flatten pepper halves with palm of hand. Coat both sides with cooking spray and cook 20 minutes or until tender, turning frequently. Place on cutting board and coarsely chop. Combine the peppers with the vinegar and 1/8 teaspoon salt, if desired. Cover to keep warm.
2. Coat both sides of the bread with cooking spray and cook 1 1/2 to 2 minutes on each side or until lightly browned. Cut each bread half crosswise into 4 pieces.
3. Top each bread slice with 1/4 cup pepper mixture and sprinkle cheese evenly over all.

Nutrition Info:
- 250 cal., 7g fat (3g sag. fat), 10mg chol, 280mg sod., 33g carb (10g sugars, 7g fiber), 12g pro.

"refried" Bean And Rice Casserole

Servings: 4 | Cooking Time:15 Minutes

Ingredients:

- 2 1/4 cups cooked brown rice (omit added salt or fat)
- 1 (15.5-ounce) can dark red kidney beans, rinsed and drained
- 7 tablespoons picante sauce
- 1/4 cup water
- 1/2 cup shredded, reduced-fat, sharp cheddar cheese

Directions:

1. Preheat the oven to 350°F.
2. Coat an 8-inch-square baking pan with nonstick cooking spray. Place the rice in the pan and set aside.
3. Add the beans, picante sauce, and water to a blender and blend until pureed, scraping the sides of the blender frequently.
4. Spread the bean mixture evenly over the rice and sprinkle with cheese. Bake, uncovered, for 15 minutes or until thoroughly heated.

Nutrition Info:

- 260 cal., 3g fat (1g sag. fat), 5mg chol, 430mg sod., 44g carb (1g sugars, 7g fiber), 14g pro.

Cauliflower Steaks With Chimichurri Sauce

Servings:4 | Cooking Time: 10 Minutes

Ingredients:

- 2 heads cauliflower (2 pounds each)
- ¼ cup extra-virgin olive oil
- Salt and pepper
- 1 recipe Chimichurri (this page)
- Lemon wedges

Directions:

1. Adjust oven rack to lowest position and heat oven to 500 degrees. Working with 1 head cauliflower at a time, discard outer leaves and trim stem flush with bottom florets. Halve cauliflower lengthwise through core. Cut one 1½-inch-thick slab lengthwise from each half, trimming any florets not connected to core. Repeat with remaining cauliflower. (You should have 4 steaks; reserve remaining cauliflower for another use.)
2. Place steaks on rimmed baking sheet and drizzle with 2 tablespoons oil. Sprinkle with pinch salt and ⅛ teaspoon pepper and rub to distribute. Flip steaks and repeat.
3. Cover sheet tightly with foil and roast for 5 minutes. Remove foil and continue to roast until bottoms of steaks are well browned, 8 to 10 minutes. Gently flip and continue to roast until cauliflower is tender and second sides are well browned, 6 to 8 minutes.
4. Transfer steaks to serving platter and brush tops evenly with ¼ cup chimichurri. Serve with lemon wedges and remaining chimichurri.

Nutrition Info:

- 370 cal., 29g fat (4g sag. fat), 0mg chol, 300mg sod., 24g carb (9g sugars, 10g fiber), 9g pro.

Chocolate Peanut Butter Parfaits

Servings: 6 | Cooking Time: 20 Minutes

Ingredients:

- 2 tablespoons reduced-fat chunky peanut butter
- 2 tablespoons plus 2 cups cold fat-free milk, divided
- 1 cup plus 6 tablespoons reduced-fat whipped topping, divided
- 1 package (1.4 ounces) sugar-free instant chocolate fudge pudding mix
- 3 tablespoons finely chopped salted peanuts

Directions:

1. In a small bowl, combine peanut butter and 2 tablespoons milk. Fold in 1 cup whipped topping; set aside. In another small bowl, whisk remaining milk with pudding mix for 2 minutes. Let stand for 2 minutes or until soft-set.
2. Spoon half of the pudding into six parfait glasses or dessert dishes. Layer with reserved peanut butter mixture and remaining pudding. Refrigerate for at least 1 hour. Refrigerate remaining whipped topping.
3. Just before serving, garnish each parfait with 1 tablespoon whipped topping and 1 1/2 teaspoons peanuts.

Nutrition Info:

- 146 cal., 6 g fat (3 g sat. fat), 2 mg chol., 300 mg sodium, 16 g carb., 1 g fiber, 6 g pro.

Tomato Topper Over Anything

Servings: 3 | Cooking Time:22 Minutes

Ingredients:

- 1 (14.5-ounce) can no-salt-added tomatoes with green pepper and onion
- 1/2 cup chopped roasted red peppers
- 2–3 tablespoons chopped fresh basil
- 2 teaspoons extra virgin olive oil

Directions:

1. Bring the tomatoes and peppers to boil in a medium saucepan. Reduce the heat and simmer, uncovered, for 15 minutes or until slightly thickened, stirring occasionally.
2. Remove the mixture from the heat, stir in the basil and oil, and let stand 5 minutes to develop flavors.

Nutrition Info:

- 80 cal., 3g fat (0g sag. fat), 0mg chol, 90mg sod., 12g carb (8g sugars, 2g fiber), 2g pro.

Speedy Greek Orzo Salad

Servings: 9 | Cooking Time:7 Minutes

Ingredients:

- 8 ounces uncooked whole-wheat orzo pasta
- 1/2 cup reduced-fat olive oil vinaigrette salad dressing (divided use)
- 3 tablespoons salt-free Greek seasoning (sold in jars in the spice aisle)
- 2 ounces crumbled, reduced-fat, sun-dried tomato and basil feta cheese
- 2 tablespoons chopped fresh parsley (optional)

Directions:

1. Cook the pasta according to package directions, omitting any salt and fat.
2. Meanwhile, stir 1/4 cup salad dressing and the Greek seasoning together in a medium bowl.
3. Drain the pasta in a colander and run under cold water until cooled. Shake off excess liquid and add it to the salad dressing mixture. Toss well, then add the feta and toss gently. Cover the bowl with plastic wrap and refrigerate at least 1 hour.
4. At serving time, add 1/4 cup salad dressing and toss to coat. Sprinkle with 2 tablespoons chopped fresh parsley, if desired.

Nutrition Info:

- 130 cal., 4g fat (1g sag. fat), 5mg chol, 180mg sod., 20g carb (1g sugars, 5g fiber), 4g pro.

Low-fat Key Lime Pie

Servings: 8 | Cooking Time: 20 Minutes

Ingredients:

- 1 package (.3 ounce) sugar-free lime gelatin
- 1/4 cup boiling water
- 2 cartons (6 ounces each) Key lime yogurt
- 1 carton (8 ounces) frozen fat-free whipped topping, thawed
- 1 reduced-fat graham cracker crust (8 inches)

Directions:

1. In a large bowl, dissolve gelatin in boiling water. Whisk in yogurt. Fold in whipped topping. Pour into crust.
2. Cover and refrigerate for at least 2 hours or until set.

Nutrition Info:

- 194 cal., 3 g fat (1 g sat. fat), 2 mg chol., 159 mg sodium, 33 g carb., 0 fiber, 3 g pro.

Iced Tea Parfaits

Servings: 4 | Cooking Time: 15 Minutes

Ingredients:

- 2 cups water
- 3 individual tea bags
- 1 package (3 ounces) lemon gelatin
- 4 maraschino cherries
- 1 1/2 cups whipped topping, divided
- 4 lemon slices

Directions:

1. In a small saucepan, bring the water to a boil. Remove from the heat; add tea bags. Cover and steep for 5 minutes. Discard the tea bags. Stir the gelatin into tea until completely dissolved. Cool slightly.
2. Pour 1/4 cup gelatin mixture into each of four parfait glasses. Place a cherry in each glass; refrigerate until set but not firm, about 1 hour. Transfer remaining gelatin mixture to a small bowl; refrigerate for 1 hour or until soft-set.
3. Whisk reserved gelatin mixture for 2-3 minutes or until smooth. Stir in 1/2 cup whipped topping; spoon into parfait glasses. Refrigerate for at least 2 hours. Just before serving, top with remaining whipped topping and garnish with lemon slices.

Nutrition Info:

- 162 cal., 5 g fat (5 g sat. fat), 0 chol., 48 mg sodium, 27 g carb., 0 fiber, 2 g pro.

Light Chocolate Truffles

Servings: 6 | Cooking Time: 25 Minutes

Ingredients:

- 1/3 cup semisweet chocolate chips
- 4 ounces reduced-fat cream cheese
- 1/3 cup plus 2 teaspoons baking cocoa, divided
- 1 1/4 cups plus 2 teaspoons confectioners' sugar, divided

Directions:

1. In a microwave, melt chocolate chips; stir until smooth. Set aside.
2. In a small bowl, beat cream cheese until fluffy. Beat in 1/3 cup cocoa and melted chocolate. Gradually beat in 1 1/4 cups confectioners' sugar. Lightly coat hands with confectioners' sugar; roll chocolate mixture into 1-in. balls. Roll in the remaining cocoa or confectioners' sugar. Cover and refrigerate for at least 1 hour.

Nutrition Info:

- 62 cal., 2 g fat (1 g sat. fat), 4 mg chol., 24 mg sodium, 11 g carb., trace fiber, 1 g pro.

Vegetables, Fruit And Side Dishes Recipes

Broccoli, Pepper And Bacon Toss

Servings: 6 | Cooking Time: 15 Minutes

Ingredients:

- 6 cups frozen broccoli florets
- 2 cups frozen stir-fry bell peppers and onions (from 1-lb bag)
- ½ cup raisins
- 2 tablespoons reduced-fat coleslaw dressing
- 2 tablespoons real bacon pieces (from 2.8-oz package)

Directions:

1. Cook broccoli and stir-fry bell peppers and onions mixture separately in microwave as directed on packages. Drain well.
2. In large bowl, toss broccoli, bell pepper mixture, raisins and coleslaw dressing. Sprinkle with bacon. Serve warm.

Nutrition Info:

- 130 cal., 2g fat (0g sat. fat), 0 chol., 70mg sod., 22g carb. (12g sugars, 5g fiber), 6g pro.

Hot Skillet Pineapple

Servings: 4 | Cooking Time:7 Minutes

Ingredients:

- 2 tablespoons no-trans-fat margarine (35% vegetable oil)
- 1 1/2 teaspoons packed dark brown sugar
- 1/2 teaspoon ground curry powder
- 8 slices pineapple packed in juice

Directions:

1. Place a large nonstick skillet over medium-high heat until hot. Add the margarine, sugar, and curry and bring to a boil. Stir to blend.
2. Arrange the pineapple slices in a single layer in the skillet. Cook 6 minutes until the pineapples are richly golden in color, turning frequently.
3. Arrange the pineapples on a serving platter and let stand 5 minutes to develop flavors and cool slightly. Serve hot or room temperature.

Nutrition Info:

- 70 cal., 2g fat (0g sag. fat), 0mg chol, 45mg sod., 13g carb (12g sugars, 1g fiber), 0g pro.

Buttery Tarragon Sugar Snaps

Servings: 4 | Cooking Time:8 Minutes

Ingredients:

- 8 ounces sugar snap peas, trimmed
- 1 1/2 tablespoons no-trans-fat margarine (35% vegetable oil)
- 1 tablespoon chopped fresh parsley
- 1/2 teaspoon dried tarragon
- 1/4 teaspoon salt

Directions:

1. Steam the sugar snaps for 6 minutes or until they are tender-crisp.
2. Place them in a serving bowl, add the remaining ingredients, and toss gently.

Nutrition Info:

- 45 cal., 2g fat (0g sag. fat), 0mg chol, 180mg sod., 5g carb (2g sugars, 1g fiber), 1g pro.

Broiled Broccoli Rabe

Servings:4 | Cooking Time:x

Ingredients:

- 3 tablespoons extra-virgin olive oil
- 1 pound broccoli rabe
- 1 garlic clove, minced
- ¼ teaspoon salt
- ¼ teaspoon red pepper flakes
- Lemon wedges

Directions:

1. Adjust oven rack 4 inches from broiler element and heat broiler. Brush rimmed baking sheet with 1 tablespoon oil.
2. Trim and discard bottom 1 inch of broccoli rabe stems. Wash broccoli rabe with cold water, then dry with clean dish towel. Cut tops (leaves and florets) from stems, then cut stems into 1-inch pieces (keep tops whole). Transfer broccoli rabe to prepared sheet.
3. Combine remaining 2 tablespoons oil, garlic, salt, and pepper flakes in small bowl. Pour oil mixture over broccoli rabe and toss to combine.
4. Broil until half of leaves are well browned, 2 to 2½ minutes. Using tongs, toss to expose unbrowned leaves. Return sheet to oven and continue to broil until most leaves are lightly charred and stems are crisp-tender, 2 to 2½ minutes. Transfer to serving platter and serve, passing lemon wedges.

Nutrition Info:

- 120 cal., 11g fat (1g sag. fat), 0mg chol, 180mg sod., 4g carb (0g sugars, 3g fiber), 4g pro.

Lemon-garlic Broccoli With Yellow Peppers

Servings: 6 | Cooking Time: 20 Minutes

Ingredients:

- 4 cups fresh broccoli florets (about 10 oz)
- ½ cup bite-size strips yellow bell pepper
- 1 tablespoon olive oil
- 1 clove garlic, finely chopped
- 1 tablespoon water
- 1 teaspoon grated lemon peel
- ¼ teaspoon salt

Directions:

1. In 3-quart saucepan, heat 4 cups water to boiling. Add broccoli; heat to boiling. Boil uncovered 2 minutes.
2. Add bell pepper; boil 1 to 2 minutes or until vegetables are crisp-tender. Drain; remove from saucepan.
3. To same saucepan, add oil and garlic. Cook over medium heat, stirring occasionally, until golden. Stir in 1 tablespoon water, the lemon peel and salt. Return broccoli mixture to saucepan; toss to coat.

Nutrition Info:

- 50 cal., 2.5g fat (0g sat. fat), 0 chol., 120mg sod., 5g carb. (1g sugars, 1g fiber), 2g pro.

Broccoli Piquant

Servings: 4 | Cooking Time:7 Minutes

Ingredients:

- 10 ounces fresh broccoli florets
- 1 tablespoon no-trans-fat margarine (35% vegetable oil)
- 1 teaspoon Worcestershire sauce
- 1 teaspoon lemon juice
- 1/4 teaspoon salt

Directions:

1. Steam the broccoli for 6 minutes or until the broccoli is tender-crisp.
2. Meanwhile, microwave the remaining ingredients in a small glass bowl on HIGH for 15 seconds. Stir until smooth.
3. Place the broccoli on a serving platter and drizzle the sauce evenly over all.

Nutrition Info:

- 35 cal., 1g fat (0g sag. fat), 0mg chol, 200mg sod., 4g carb (2g sugars, 2g fiber), 2g pro.

Confetti Corn

Servings:4 | Cooking Time: 15 Minutes

Ingredients:

- 1/4 cup chopped carrot
- 1 tablespoon olive oil
- 2 3/4 cups fresh or frozen corn, thawed
- 1/4 cup chopped water chestnuts
- 1/4 cup chopped sweet red pepper

Directions:

1. In a large skillet, saute the carrot in oil until crisp-tender. Stir in the corn, water chestnuts and red pepper; heat until warmed through.

Nutrition Info:

- 140 cal., 4g fat (1g sat. fat), 0 chol., 7mg sod., 26g carb. (3g sugars, 3g fiber), 4g pro.

Cran-orange Swiss Chard

Servings: 4 | Cooking Time: 25 Minutes

Ingredients:

- 1 medium onion, sliced
- 1 tablespoon olive oil
- 10 cups chopped Swiss chard
- 1/4 cup orange juice
- 2 tablespoons dried cranberries
- Dash salt and pepper
- 2 tablespoons coarsely chopped walnuts, toasted

Directions:

1. In a large skillet, saute onion in oil until tender. Add chard; saute for 3-5 minutes or just until wilted.
2. Stir in the orange juice, cranberries, salt and pepper; cook for 1-2 minutes or until cranberries are softened. Sprinkle with walnuts.

Nutrition Info:

- 104 cal., 6 g fat (1 g sat. fat), 0 chol., 230 mg sodium, 12 g carb., 3 g fiber, 3 g pro.

Pan-roasted Broccoli

Servings:6 | Cooking Time:10minutes

Ingredients:

- ¼ teaspoon salt
- ⅛ teaspoon pepper
- 2 tablespoons extra-virgin olive oil
- 1¾ pounds broccoli, florets cut into 1½-inch pieces, stalks peeled and cut on bias into ¼-inch-thick slices

Directions:

1. Stir 3 tablespoons water, salt, and pepper together in small bowl until salt dissolves; set aside. Heat oil in 12-inch nonstick skillet over medium-high heat until just smoking. Add broccoli stalks in even layer and cook, without stirring, until browned on bottoms, about 2 minutes. Add florets to skillet and toss to combine. Cook, without stirring, until bottoms of florets just begin to brown, 1 to 2 minutes.
2. Add water mixture and cover skillet. Cook until broccoli is bright green but still crisp, about 2 minutes. Uncover and continue to cook until water has evaporated, broccoli stalks are tender, and florets are crisp-tender, about 2 minutes. Serve.

Nutrition Info:

- 70 cal., 5g fat (0g sag. fat), 0mg chol, 125mg sod., 5g carb (1g sugars, 2g fiber), 2g pro.

Spicy Green Beans With Caramelized Onions

Servings: 8 | Cooking Time: 25 Minutes

Ingredients:

- 1 tablespoon olive oil
- 1 tablespoon sugar
- 1 large white onion, thinly sliced (1½ cups)
- 1 lb fresh green beans, trimmed
- 2 tablespoons reduced-sodium soy sauce
- ½ teaspoon salt
- ½ teaspoon crushed red pepper flakes

Directions:

1. In 10-inch skillet, heat oil and sugar over medium heat, stirring occasionally. Add onion; cook 10 to 15 minutes, stirring frequently, until tender and light golden brown. Remove onion from skillet.
2. To same skillet, add remaining ingredients. Cook 3 to 5 minutes, stirring constantly, until beans are crisp-tender. Stir in onion; cook until thoroughly heated.

Nutrition Info:

- 50 cal., 2g fat (0g sat. fat), 0 chol., 280mg sod., 8g carb. (4g sugars, 2g fiber), 1g pro.

Grilled Summer Squash

Servings: 4 | Cooking Time: 25 Minutes

Ingredients:
- 2 medium yellow summer squash, sliced
- 2 medium sweet red peppers, sliced
- 1 large sweet onion, halved and sliced
- 2 tablespoons olive oil
- 2 garlic cloves, minced
- 1 teaspoon sugar
- 1/4 teaspoon salt
- 1/4 teaspoon pepper

Directions:

1. In a large bowl, combine all the ingredients. Divide between two double thicknesses of heavy-duty foil (about 18 in. x 12 in.). Fold foil around vegetable mixture and seal tightly.

2. Grill, covered, over medium heat for 10-15 minutes or until vegetables are tender. Open foil carefully to allow steam to escape.

Nutrition Info:
- 124 cal., 7 g fat (1 g sat. fat), 0 chol., 159 mg sodium, 15 g carb., 3 g fiber, 3 g pro.

Roasted Beets

Servings:4 | Cooking Time:60 Minutes

Ingredients:
- 1½ pounds beets, trimmed
- 1 tablespoon extra-virgin olive oil
- 1 tablespoon sherry vinegar
- 1 tablespoon minced fresh parsley
- Salt and pepper

Directions:

1. Adjust oven rack to middle position and heat oven to 400 degrees. Wrap beets individually in aluminum foil and place on rimmed baking sheet. Roast beets until skewer inserted into center meets little resistance (you will need to unwrap beets to test them), 45 to 60 minutes.

2. Remove beets from oven and slowly open foil packets (being careful of rising steam). When beets are cool enough to handle but still warm, gently rub off skins using paper towels.

3. Slice beets into ½-inch-thick wedges, then toss with oil, vinegar, parsley, and ¼ teaspoon salt. Season with pepper to taste and serve warm or at room temperature. (Beets can be refrigerated for up to 3 days; return to room temperature before serving.)

Nutrition Info:
- 80 cal., 3g fat (0g sag. fat), 0mg chol, 240mg sod., 11g carb (8g sugars, 3g fiber), 2g pro.

Roasted Cauliflower

Servings:6 | Cooking Time:20 Minutes

Ingredients:

- 1 head cauliflower (2 pounds)
- ¼ cup extra-virgin olive oil
- Salt and pepper

Directions:

1. Adjust oven rack to lowest position and heat oven to 475 degrees. Line a rimmed baking sheet with aluminum foil. Trim outer leaves off cauliflower and cut stem flush with bottom of head. Cut head into 8 equal wedges. Place wedges, with either cut side down, on lined baking sheet, drizzle with 2 tablespoons oil, and sprinkle with ¼ teaspoon salt and ⅛ teaspoon pepper. Gently rub oil and seasonings into cauliflower. Gently flip cauliflower and repeat on second cut side with remaining 2 tablespoons oil, ¼ teaspoon salt, and ⅛ teaspoon pepper.
2. Cover baking sheet tightly with foil and roast for 10 minutes. Remove foil and continue to roast until bottoms of cauliflower wedges are golden, 8 to 12 minutes.
3. Remove sheet from oven, carefully flip wedges using spatula, and continue to roast until cauliflower is golden all over, 8 to 12 minutes. Transfer to serving dish, season with pepper to taste, and serve.

Nutrition Info:

- 120 cal., 10g fat (1g sag. fat), 0mg chol, 240mg sod., 8g carb (3g sugars, 3g fiber), 3g pro.

Crunchy Pear And Cilantro Relish

Servings: 4 | Cooking Time: 6 Minutes

Ingredients:

- 2 firm medium pears, peeled, cored, and finely chopped (about 1/4-inch cubes)
- 3/4 teaspoon lime zest
- 3 tablespoons lime juice
- 1 1/4 tablespoons sugar
- 3 tablespoons chopped cilantro or mint

Directions:

1. Place all ingredients in a bowl and toss well.
2. Serve immediately for peak flavor and texture.

Nutrition Info:

- 50 cal., 0g fat (0g sag. fat), 0mg chol, 0mg sod., 14g carb (9g sugars, 3g fiber), 0g pro.

Hearty Beans And Rice

Servings: 5 | Cooking Time: 25 Minutes

Ingredients:

- 1 pound lean ground beef (90% lean)
- 1 can (15 ounces) black beans, rinsed and drained
- 1 can (14 1/2 ounces) diced tomatoes with mild green chilies, undrained
- 1 1/3 cups frozen corn, thawed
- 1 cup water
- 1/4 teaspoon salt
- 1 1/2 cups instant brown rice

Directions:

1. In a large saucepan, cook beef over medium heat until no longer pink; drain. Stir in the beans, tomatoes, corn, water and salt. Bring to a boil. Stir in rice; return to a boil. Reduce heat; cover and simmer for 5 minutes. Remove from the heat; let stand, covered, for 5 minutes.

Nutrition Info:

- 376 cal., 9 g fat (3 g sat. fat), 56 mg chol., 647 mg sodium, 47 g carb., 7 g fiber, 26 g pro.

Sautéed Cabbage With Parsley And Lemon

Servings:6 | Cooking Time:x

Ingredients:

- 1 small head green cabbage (1¼ pounds), cored and sliced thin
- 2 tablespoons extra-virgin olive oil
- 1 onion, halved and sliced thin
- Salt and pepper
- ¼ cup chopped fresh parsley
- 1½ teaspoons lemon juice

Directions:

1. Place cabbage in large bowl and cover with cold water. Let sit for 3 minutes; drain well.
2. Heat 1 tablespoon oil in 12-inch nonstick skillet over medium-high heat until shimmering. Add onion and ¼ teaspoon salt and cook until softened and lightly browned, 5 to 7 minutes; transfer to bowl.
3. Heat remaining 1 tablespoon oil in now-empty skillet over medium-high heat until shimmering. Add cabbage and sprinkle with ¼ teaspoon salt and ¼ teaspoon pepper. Cover and cook, without stirring, until cabbage is wilted and lightly browned on bottom, about 3 minutes. Stir and continue to cook, uncovered, until cabbage is crisp-tender and lightly browned in places, about 4 minutes, stirring once halfway through cooking. Off heat, stir in onion, parsley, and lemon juice. Season with pepper to taste and serve.

Nutrition Info:

- 80 cal., 4g fat (0g sag. fat), 0mg chol, 220mg sod., 8g carb (4g sugars, 3g fiber), 1g pro.

Roasted Sesame Asparagus

Servings: 4 | Cooking Time: 15 Minutes

Ingredients:

- 1 lb fresh asparagus spears (about 16)
- 1 tablespoon dark sesame oil
- 1 teaspoon soy sauce
- ½ teaspoon wasabi paste
- ¼ teaspoon black or white sesame seed

Directions:

1. Heat oven to 450°F. Break off tough ends of asparagus as far down as stalks snap easily. In ungreased 15 × 10 × 1-inch pan, place asparagus spears in single layer.
2. In small bowl, mix remaining ingredients except sesame seed; pour over asparagus, turning asparagus to coat evenly.
3. Roast 8 to 10 minutes or until asparagus is crisp-tender (asparagus will appear slightly charred). Sprinkle with sesame seed.

Nutrition Info:

- 50 cal., 3.5g fat (0.5g sat. fat), 0 chol., 75mg sod., 2g carb. (1g sugars, 1g fiber), 1g pro.

Easy Baked Mushrooms

Servings: 4 | Cooking Time: 30 Minutes

Ingredients:

- 1 pound medium fresh mushrooms, halved
- 2 tablespoons olive oil
- 1/4 cup seasoned bread crumbs
- 1/4 teaspoon garlic powder
- 1/4 teaspoon pepper
- Fresh parsley, optional

Directions:

1. Place mushrooms on a baking sheet. Drizzle with oil; toss to coat. In a small bowl, combine the bread crumbs, garlic powder and pepper; sprinkle over the mushrooms.
2. Bake, uncovered, at 425° for 18-20 minutes or until lightly browned. Garnish with parsley if desired.

Nutrition Info:

- 116 cal., 8 g fat (1 g sat. fat), 0 chol., 112 mg sodium, 10 g carb., 2 g fiber, 4 g pro.

Grilled Soy Pepper Petites

Servings: 4 | Cooking Time:12 Minutes

Ingredients:

- 1 pound petite peppers
- 3 tablespoons apricot or raspberry fruit spread
- 1 1/2 tablespoons light soy sauce
- 1/8 to 1/4 teaspoon dried pepper flakes

Directions:

1. Heat a grill or grill pan over medium-high heat. Coat peppers with cooking spray and cook 12 minutes or until tender and beginning to char, turning frequently.
2. Meanwhile, heat fruit spread in microwave for 15 seconds to melt slightly; whisk in soy sauce and pepper flakes.
3. Place peppers in a shallow bowl or rimmed platter and toss with mixture. Serve warm or room temperature.

Nutrition Info:

- 55 cal., 0g fat (0g sag. fat), 0mg chol, 200mg sod., 12g carb (9g sugars, 2g fiber), 2g pro.

Squash Melt

Servings: 4 | Cooking Time:8 Minutes

Ingredients:

- 2 medium yellow squash (about 12 ounces total), cut in 1/8-inch rounds
- 1 medium green bell pepper, chopped or 1 cup thinly sliced yellow onion
- 1/4–1/2 teaspoon dried oregano
- 1/4 teaspoon salt
- 1/4 cup shredded, reduced-fat, sharp cheddar cheese

Directions:

1. Place a medium nonstick skillet over medium-high heat until hot. Coat the skillet with nonstick cooking spray and add all the ingredients except the cheese.
2. Coat the vegetables with nonstick cooking spray and cook 6–7 minutes or until the vegetables are tender, stirring constantly. Use two utensils to stir as you would when stir-frying.
3. Remove the skillet from the heat and sprinkle the vegetables evenly with the cheese. Cover and let stand 2 minutes to melt the cheese.

Nutrition Info:

- 40 cal., 1g fat (0g sag. fat), 5mg chol, 190mg sod., 5g carb (3g sugars, 2g fiber), 3g pro.

Fresh Lemon Roasted Brussels Sprouts

Servings: 4 | Cooking Time:20 Minutes

Ingredients:

- 1 pound fresh Brussels sprouts, ends trimmed and halved
- 2 tablespoons extra-virgin olive oil, divided
- Juice and zest of 1 medium lemon
- 2 teaspoons Worcestershire sauce
- 1/4 teaspoon pepper

Directions:

1. Preheat oven 425°F.
2. Toss Brussels sprouts with 1 tablespoon oil, place in a single layer on a foil-lined baking sheet. Roast 10 minutes, stir, and cook 10 minutes or until just tender and beginning to brown.
3. Remove, toss with remaining ingredients and 1/4 teaspoon salt, if desired.

Nutrition Info:

- 115 cal., 7g fat (1g sag. fat), 0mg chol, 55mg sod., 13g carb (3g sugars, 5g fiber), 4g pro.

Sesame Broccoli

Servings: 6 | Cooking Time: 25 Minutes

Ingredients:

- 1 pound fresh broccoli, cut into spears
- 1 tablespoon reduced-sodium soy sauce
- 2 teaspoons olive oil
- 2 teaspoons balsamic vinegar
- 1 1/2 teaspoons honey
- 2 teaspoons sesame seeds, toasted

Directions:

1. Place broccoli in a steamer basket; place in a saucepan over 1 in. of water. Bring to a boil; cover and steam for 10-15 minutes or until crisp-tender. Meanwhile, in a small saucepan, combine the soy sauce, oil, vinegar and honey; cook and stir over medium-low heat until heated through.
2. Transfer broccoli to a serving bowl; drizzle with soy sauce mixture. Sprinkle with sesame seeds.

Nutrition Info:

- 48 cal., 2 g fat (trace sat. fat), 0 chol., 127 mg sodium, 6 g carb., 2 g fiber, 3 g pro.

Broiled Eggplant With Basil

Servings:6 | Cooking Time:9 Minutes

Ingredients:

- 1½ pounds eggplant, sliced into ¼-inch-thick rounds
- Kosher salt and pepper
- 3 tablespoons extra-virgin olive oil
- 2 tablespoons chopped fresh basil

Directions:

1. Spread eggplant on paper towel–lined baking sheet, sprinkle both sides with 1½ teaspoons salt, and let sit for 9 minutes.
2. Adjust oven rack 4 inches from broiler element and heat broiler. Thoroughly pat eggplant dry with paper towels, arrange on aluminum foil–lined rimmed baking sheet in single layer, and brush both sides with oil. Broil eggplant until mahogany brown and lightly charred, about 4 minutes per side. Transfer eggplant to serving platter, season with pepper to taste, and sprinkle with basil. Serve.

Nutrition Info:

- 90 cal., 7g fat (1g sag. fat), 0mg chol, 140mg sod., 7g carb (4g sugars, 3g fiber), 1g pro.

Appendix : Recipes Index

H

I

L

M

N

T

W

Y

Z

Printed in Great Britain
by Amazon

22988367R00051